W9-BXV-752

THE POLITICS OF
DICTATORSHIP

THE POLITICS OF
DICTATORSHIP

Institutions and Outcomes in Authoritarian Regimes

Erica Frantz
Natasha Ezrow

LYNNE
RIENNER
PUBLISHERS

BOULDER
LONDON

Published in the United States of America in 2011 by
Lynne Rienner Publishers, Inc.
1800 30th Street, Boulder, Colorado 80301
www.rienner.com

and in the United Kingdom by
Lynne Rienner Publishers, Inc.
3 Henrietta Street, Covent Garden, London WC2E 8LU

Library of Congress Cataloging-in-Publication Data
Frantz, Erica.
The politics of dictatorship : institutions and outcomes in authoritarian regimes
/ by Erica Frantz and Natasha Ezrow.
    p.   cm.
Includes bibliographical references and index.
ISBN 978-1-58826-785-6 (hardcover : alk. paper)
1. Dictatorship. 2. Dictators. 3. Authoritarianism. I. Ezrow, Natasha M. II. Title.
JC495.F64 2011
321.9—dc22

                                                                    2010038598

British Cataloguing in Publication Data
A Cataloguing in Publication record for this book
is available from the British Library.

Printed and bound in the United States of America

The paper used in this publication meets the requirements
∞ of the American National Standard for Permanence of
Paper for Printed Library Materials Z39.48-1992.

5 4 3 2 1

Contents

Tables and Figures

Tables

Figure

1

Authoritarian Politics in the Modern World

Dictators ride to and fro upon tigers from which they dare not dismount.
—Winston Churchill ("Armistice or Peace?" 1937)

Dictators have dominated the world's political landscape for hundreds of years, ranging from the pharaohs of ancient Egypt, to the emperors of Rome, to the absolute monarchs of Europe. Indeed, authoritarian government has been the norm for much of history. And dictatorships are by no means a thing of the past. As late as the 1970s, autocracy was more common than democracy. In 2010, about one-third of the world's countries were governed by dictatorship. The Chinese communist regime alone rules nearly a quarter of the world's population (Brooker 2000, p. 1). As reported in *The Economist* in 2008: "following a decades-long global trend in democratization, the spread of democracy has come to a halt" ("Democracy Index: Off the March" 2008). Even though dictatorships are so widespread, authoritarian rule remains one of the least-studied areas of political science.[1] In comparison to democratic political systems, we know very little about how dictatorships work, who the key political actors are, and where the locus of decisionmaking rests.

The purpose of this study is to examine how authoritarianism influences political outcomes. In dictatorships, politics centers on an interplay between two key actors: leaders and elites. These actors engage in a constant struggle for power, driven by a desire for political influence. Not only do elites compete with the dictator, but they also compete with one another.[2] Authoritarian institutions shape the dynamics of this struggle. In particular, how dictatorships are governed, whether by a professionalized military, a political party, or neither, influences the nature of leader-elite relations and, in turn, how politics works. In this study, we show how these institutional differences affect a wide array of political outcomes, such as how hard it is for elites to oust dictators, the ability of elites to hold dictators accountable for poor policy choices, the quality of information channels that exist between leaders and elites, and the ease with which leaders and elites can reach agreements on significant policy changes.

The Role of Elites

We begin this study by discussing the key role that elites play in authoritarian politics. All political leaders need the support of some citizens in order to maintain their command. In dictatorships, the set of individuals whose support the dictator requires to stay in power is the elite coalition. As Paul Lewis wrote: "Regardless of how powerful dictators are, the complexities of modern society and government make it impossible for them to rule alone. They may dominate their respective systems, but some of their authority must be delegated, which means that a government elite stratum is formed just below them" (1978, p. 622). Elites matter because they control the fates of dictators. Perhaps surprisingly, the vast majority of dictators are toppled via internal coups rather than by popular uprisings (Tullock 1987). In fact, dictators are removed from power most frequently by government insiders (Svolik 2009, p. 478). As King Sesostris of Egypt was rumored to have warned future kings in 1965 B.C.E.: "Be on your guard against all subordinates, because you cannot be sure who is plotting against you" (Rindova and Starbuck 1997, p. 321). The dictator's elite support group plays a key role in authoritarian politics because the dictator's tenure is often contingent upon it.[3]

Examples of elites' role in the downfall of dictators abound. In Argentina in 1981, the leader of the military dictatorship, Roberto Viola, was overthrown by junta members because they were upset that he had established a dialogue with union leaders and included civilians in the cabinet. Similarly, in Nigeria in 1975, Yakubu Gowon was overthrown by his colleagues because they felt that he was too indecisive and no longer consulted with members of the Supreme Military Council. In Thailand in 1977, Prime Minister Tanin Kraivixien was forced to resign because elites did not like his economic policies (Tamada 1995, p. 321). Ghana provides yet another example, where in 1978, due to a steady erosion of power, Ignatius Kutu Acheampong was arrested by his chief of staff, Frederick Akuffo, who later replaced him as head of state and leader ("Background Note: Ghana" 2008). As Jean-Bédel Bokassa of the Central African Republic knew well, the greatest danger to his power came not from the opposition, but from his own entourage (Titley 1997, p. 43). Elites serve as the dictator's main political rivals and therefore primary source of political insecurity.

The Role of Party and Military Institutions

Whether dictatorships are governed by a political party, a professionalized military, or neither affects the dynamics of leader and elite interactions.[4] We emphasize party and military organizations because they are institutions that can potentially structure elite politics. Parties and militaries are forms of human organization and resource concentration that make possible the seizure of power. Unlike many other institutions, parties and militaries are largely self-enforcing bargains, because those who belong to them benefit from their membership.

We look at how political outcomes differ across the following types of dictatorship: single-party, military, and personalist.[5] These categorizations are based on whether access to political office and control over policy are dominated by a hegemonic party, the military as an institution, or a single individual. In single-party regimes, the elite coalition is usually the ruling body of the party, sometimes called the central committee or politburo; in military regimes, the coalition generally consists of the military junta (and often other high-ranked officers); and in personalist regimes, the coalition is typically made up of individuals personally chosen by the ruler. Whether the dictatorship is party-based, military-based, or neither has profound implications for the political outcomes that result, from how easy it is for dictators to survive in office to the freedom dictators have in their foreign and domestic policy choices.

Political Survival in Dictatorships

These different institutions shape the interplay between leaders and elites in their struggle for political influence, a struggle that is driven by the larger goal of political survival. Research on political survival in modern dictatorial regimes has typically emphasized the various strategies dictators employ to stay in power (Friedrich and Brzezinski 1956; Arendt 1951; Tullock 1987).[6] In Mancur Olson's (2000) conceptualization, for example, dictators come to power as stationary bandits who monopolize and rationalize theft in the form of taxes. The time horizons of dictators influence the extent to which they will provide a peaceful order and other public goods that increase the productivity of their subjects. Olson's story, however, assumes that dictators do not face any threats to their survival once in power. Ronald Wintrobe's (1998) argument emphasizes this point. Dictators are inherently insecure because they never know whether their subjects are their allies or their rivals. Some analysts note that dictators face the constant threat of popular rebellion (see Acemoglu and Robinson 2001; Boix 2003; Sanhueza 1999). To deter this threat, dictators have a variety of tools at their disposal, such as repressing some parts of the population while nurturing the loyalty of others (Wintrobe 1998) and incorporating potential opposition forces in the regime via partisan legislatures (Gandhi and Przeworski 2007). This emphasis on the threat of popular uprising, however, is somewhat misguided. Empirically, the primary threat to the leader's tenure is not popular rebellion or revolution. As Malawian personalist dictator Hastings Banda was aware, "danger to [the leader's] rule comes not from any likely popular uprising, but from a 'palace coup' within his own ruling party" (Legum 1975–1976, B268). This is not to say that the threat of revolution does not exist, but rather that dictators are ousted far more frequently by members of their own inner circle than by members of opposition groups.

Various scholars acknowledge this and address explicitly the threats dictators face from within their ruling coalition (Svolik 2009; Gallego and Pitchik 2004; Egorov and Sonin 2006). According to Bruce Bueno de Mesquita and colleagues (2003), for example, there are two key groups that influence leaders' political survival: the selectorate (a subset of the population that has a say in the selection of the leader) and the winning coalition (a subset of the selectorate large enough to maintain a leader in power). The leader's position is the most secure when the selectorate is large and the winning coalition is small. This is partly because the costs of defection can be high in such situations, but also because members of the winning coalition can easily be replaced by members of the selectorate. Though the concepts underlying this theory are useful, the argument is difficult to evaluate given that in most dictatorships it is not clear who the selectorate is. Which individuals in authoritarian regimes, apart from members of the winning coalition, actually have a say in the selection of dictators? In military dictatorships, for example, elites and leaders typically rely on other members of the military for the regime to last. These low-level members of the military, however, rarely, if ever, have any say in the selection of leaders.[7]

In a different vein, Beatriz Magaloni argues that in order to survive in office, dictators need to establish "power-sharing agreements with their ruling coalitions, which are often not credible" (2008, p. 715). Because there is nothing that prevents dictators from reneging on their commitments to those in their support group, potential rivals have incentives to conspire or rebel. To mitigate this commitment problem, dictators choose to share some of their power with members of their ruling coalition, primarily via the creation of political parties and elections. This argument, however, essentially assumes that dictators inherit structure-free domestic environments upon their assumption to power, and create from scratch any institutional arrangements that emerge. Jennifer Gandhi and Adam Przeworski (2007) make a similar assumption. The extent to which such an assumption will be true, though, will depend on how tightly organized the seizure group is that launched the dictator into power. As Stephen Haber writes: "Dictators need an organized group in order to take power. Some of these groups, such as the military, a political party, or a royal family, are formally constituted, have rules governing their internal workings, and may already be part of a pre-existing government. Others, such as a revolutionary movement, a military splinter group, or a federation of warlords are less institutionalized" (2006, p. 6). The more formally constituted the seizure group is, the more likely it is that the regime that forms will share structural characteristics similar to those of the seizure group, and the more difficult it will be for the leader at the helm of the group to mold the structure of the regime in ways that will prolong his political survival (Geddes 2004). In addition, leadership turnover within the same regime is very common (discussed in more detail in Chapter 2). In such scenarios, leaders inherit whatever institutional structures (or lack thereof) that precede them. Dictators may try to alter these structures, but their success in doing so is in no way guaranteed.

This study expands on past work on political survival in dictatorships by emphasizing that (1) elites are the primary threat to the dictator's survival, and (2) domestic institutions shape the severity of the threat they pose.

Regime Formation and Institutional Change

The foundational moments of authoritarian regimes usually have lasting effects on their institutional structures. Whether dictatorships are party-based, military-based, or neither typically results from struggles within the seizure group, often at the time of seizure or during the first few years afterward (Geddes 2004; Haber 2006, p. 21). Once the seizure group takes control, its leader tries to maximize his power and personalize the regime, while the group's members work to resist such efforts (Geddes 2004). The result of this strategic interaction—largely determined by the group's preexisting organizational strength—has profound implications for the makeup of the emergent regime. Put simply, when seizure groups are organizationally strong, members are able to prevent personalization (resulting in military or single-party regimes); when seizure groups are organizationally weak, members are unable to formidably challenge the leader's efforts and the group dissolves or splinters (resulting in personalist regimes). Military dictatorships, for example, are usually the result of seizures of power undertaken by military hierarchies that are more professionalized, having "developed more binding commitments to military norms of unity, obedience, and rule-boundedness than have less professionalized or recently indigenized militaries" (Geddes 2004, p. 22). Similarly, single-party dictatorships are usually the result of seizures of power undertaken by parties that are more professionalized, having "led revolutionary struggles or resistance to foreign occupation than those in less demanding circumstances" (Geddes 2004, p. 22). When seizure groups lack such professionalization, personalist forms of dictatorship tend to emerge.[8]

Leaders' attempts to maximize their power do not stop once regimes are formed, of course. Because all leaders have the same goal—to stay in power for as long as possible (Tullock 1987)—most will try to gain personal control over as many key political instruments as possible throughout their tenures, such as control over assignments to political posts, control over policy, and control over the security forces.[9] Once established, however, institutional structures can be hard to change. In East Germany, for example, Walter Ulbricht tried to increase his power through party purges and expulsions. His success, however, was limited by opposition from other members of his party (Granville 2006). This does not mean that institutional structures do not change, but rather that they can develop stickiness over time.[10]

The emergence of new organizations in dictatorships does not always reflect a significant change in the institutional structure of the regime, however. This is particularly true with political parties. It is very common for dictatorships to co-opt or create a political party to support the regime (Geddes 2005). Examples include Rafael Trujillo's alliance with the Dominican Party during his personalist reign over the Dominican Republic (1966–1978) and the Brazilian military dictatorship's (1964–1985) creation of the National Renewal Alliance Party (ARENA) in 1966. As many studies have identified (Gandhi and Przeworski 2006; Gandhi 2008; Brownlee 2008; Geddes 2005), dictatorships create political parties (or ally with existing ones) because support parties contain real benefits for the regime and can help prolong its hold on power. A regime's decision to create or ally with a political party, however, should not be conflated as a transition to party-based rule. That a party is represented in government does not mean that it exercises any independent political power, has a say in leadership selection, or plays a significant role in distributing patronage to supporters (Magaloni and Kricheli 2010, p. 126; Geddes 2003, p. 52), all of which are key characteristics of party-based dictatorship. Though it is typical for regimes to create or ally with political parties as survival tools, such parties are usually kept organizationally weak and dependent on the regime to ensure that they do not develop any real power or autonomy. Their incorporation into the regime should not be seen as fundamentally altering the regime's structure or power base.

Still, authoritarian regimes are nearly always characterized by some level of institutional fluidity. This fluidity is the result of the endless power struggle at play between elites and dictators that we emphasize throughout this study. While it occasionally translates into a fundamental transformation of the institutional structure of the regime (i.e., regime change), it is generally just part of the natural ebb and flow of authoritarian politics. Even amid this institutional fluidity, the central theoretical mechanisms that we identify in this study should still operate.[11]

Key Themes

Woven throughout our exploration of how the institutional structure of dictatorships influences the nature of the relationship between dictators and their elite supporters and, in turn, influences how politics works, is an emphasis on two key dimensions. These dimensions each affect how power is distributed between leaders and elites. The first is whether elites share membership in a unifying institution (central to Chapters 2, 3, 4, and 5). When elites share membership in a unifying institution, like a party or military, it enables them to bargain with the dictator as a collective. This eases coordination barriers among elites, increasing their bargaining power relative to the dictator and making it more difficult for dictators to appoint and dismiss coalition members at will. The second dimension is whether elites have control over the security forces (central to Chapters 2 and 3). When elites have control over the security forces, it gives them access to troops and weaponry. This increases their ability to carry out a coup and makes it easier for elites to unseat the dictator.

Chapter 2 examines both of these dimensions in more detail, laying out the key theoretical arguments from which we build throughout the study. The chapter focuses on how the institutional structure of dictatorships affects leadership survival. We contend that it is easiest for elites to unseat leaders in military dictatorships, followed by single-party dictatorships, and lastly personalist dictatorships. Military leaders face the highest risk of being overthrown by their erstwhile supporters both because the preexisting hierarchical organization of the military helps coalition members overcome coordination problems and also because coalition members control arms and troops. At the other extreme, personalist leaders face few credible threats of overthrow. Their supporters, far from being organized into a preexisting structure that can help to overcome coordination problems, often compete with one another for the leader's favor. Personalist dictators select members of their coalition at will and choose individuals who pose little threat to their continued rule. In single-party regimes, the party organization reduces the costs of coordination but does not give members of the elite coalition access to the physical means to overthrow the leader by force. We test our expectation by examining leadership survival rates across dictatorships.

Chapter 3 examines how the makeup of dictatorships affects the likelihood that regimes will be participants in escalatory cross-border conflicts. To generate expectations about what dictatorships in different institutional settings will do, we look at how dictators differ in their ability to show their resolve during interstate disputes. In democracies, when leaders make public threats, and then back down, voters punish them for having done so. By going public with their demands, democratic leaders establish a hands-tying mechanism, creating domestic costs that they would suffer if they fail to follow through with their threats. In dictatorships, since ordinary citizens cannot routinely oust dictators, the ability of dictators to show that their threats are credible depends on how well elites can threaten to overthrow the dictator for poor foreign policy choices. Because military leaders face a greater risk of being ousted by their elite support group (as we show in Chapter 2), they should be the most capable of generating high domestic costs for backing down on their threats, followed by single-party dictators, and lastly personalist dictators. Consequently, target states should perceive threats from military dictators to be more credible than those from personalist or single-party dictators, because they know that military leaders will face a high probability of being ousted if they fail after issuing a challenge. Target states back down in disputes when they perceive the threat to be credible (Schultz 1999; Prins 2003; Weeks 2008). Therefore, when military dictators threaten other states, the dispute should be less likely to escalate. We test this expectation by looking at the likelihood that conflict will escalate given the regime type of the state that provokes it.

Chapter 4 extends this analysis and examines how the institutional structure of the dictatorship influences the ability of dictators to accurately judge the credibility of threats sent by their adversaries. In order for signaling advantages to matter, as claimed by James Fearon (1994) and others, target states must be able to correctly identify when signals are credible. Leaders' ability to accurately read signals depends on the quality of the military intelligence that they receive. With low-quality intelligence, leaders are more likely to misread signals and make foreign policy errors. In dictatorships, leaders receive information on security matters from their elite advisory group. Paradoxically, when leaders have more power over the composition of this group, it decreases the caliber of military intelligence they receive. Leaders select individuals who are less likely to overthrow them, but who are also less competent. Elites who are entirely dependent on the dictator will refrain from reporting any information the dictator does not want to hear, out of fear of reprisal. As we discuss in Chapter 2, because personalist dictators do not bargain with a unified support group, they have greater control over selection to the advisory group and are often able to remove anyone with the ability to challenge their rule. Consequently, their advisory group is more likely to exclude those who might also provide them with the most sophisticated advice. In military and single-party dictatorships, by contrast, elites usually have to work their way up the party or military ladder to reach their positions. As a result, they are typically better-trained than are their counterparts in personalist dictatorships, where elites tend to be friends or family members of the dictator. We argue that in comparison to other dictators, personalist dictators should be more likely to receive low-quality information from their subordinates and, as a result, more likely to misread threats sent by their adversaries. We test this by examining the likelihood that dictators will misread signals sent to them during foreign policy disputes and commit foreign policy errors.

Chapter 5 looks at how the institutional makeup of dictatorships makes it easier or more difficult for dictators to enact significant policy changes. Policies in dictatorships essentially require the tacit support of two actors: the dictator and the elite support coalition. In many ways, the role of each of these two actors is analogous to that of a veto player. That is, the leader of the regime acts as an individual veto player, and the elite coalition functions as a collective veto player. We argue that the makeup of the collective veto player differs fundamentally across dictatorships. As we discuss in Chapters 2 and 4, personalist dictators have a greater say in the selection of their elite supporters than do military or single-party dictators (since no autonomous party or military institution controls elite recruitment). Because of this, they can select individuals whose preferences mirror their own and eliminate any who resist policy change. In personalist dictatorships, the collective veto player shares the ideal preference point of the individual veto player, making it easier for the two to agree on policy. Military and single-party dictators do not have this liberty and cannot ensure that their support coalition is predominantly comprised of those individuals who agree with them. Even though they can usually eliminate a few opponents, they cannot arbitrarily replace all members of their support group as personalist rulers can. In military and single-party dictatorships, the collective veto player is somewhat ideologically heterogeneous (even in ideologically dogmatic regimes) and does not always share the ideal preference point of the individual veto player. This makes it more difficult for the two players to reach agreements on policy, reducing the likelihood of large swings in policy. Therefore, we expect that military and single-party dictatorships will exhibit the most policy stability and personalist dictatorships the least. We test this by examining how easy or hard it is for dictatorships to enact big policy changes.

Concluding our study, Chapter 6 emphasizes how the institutional structure of dictatorships in many ways determines the behavior of authoritarian regimes and the political outcomes that result. Whether dictatorships are party-based, military-based, or neither largely defines the nature of leader-elite interactions and, consequently, influences politics. Institutional differences across dictatorships help to explain multiple political outcomes, such as why some dictatorships are more likely to escalate interstate conflicts, why some dictatorships are more likely to enact dramatic policy changes, and why some dictators seem to rule forever while others are easily overthrown.

Conclusion

The internal architecture of autocracies plays a key role in shaping the relationship between leaders and their elite supporters. Understanding how the institutional makeup of dictatorships affects the nature of leader-elite relations not only aids in the development of our theoretical understanding of autocratic politics, but also has serious foreign policy implications. Given the persistent centrality of notorious dictatorships to the foreign policy agendas of many of the world's states, identifying who the key actors are in dictatorships and the ways in which they are politically vulnerable is of fundamental importance.

This study is informed by influential work in the field of authoritarian politics that examines how internal struggles for power are shaped by differing institutional contexts (such as Gandhi and Przeworski 2007; Geddes 2003, 2004; Haber 2006; Lust-Okar 2005; Magaloni 2006). The theoretical mechanisms that we propose, while deeply rooted in this body of research, expand its scope considerably by generating a wide array of testable expectations for how authoritarianism affects both domestic and international political outcomes. These mechanisms are remarkably simple and based on just two key dimensions: whether elites share membership in a unifying institution and whether elites have control over the security forces. By identifying shortcuts for understanding political processes in dictatorships, this study helps to reduce some of the mystery that shrouds these regimes, enabling broad advancements in our understanding of them to crystallize and come to the fore.

Notes

1. As Adam Przeworski recently noted: "Dictatorships are by far the most understudied area in comparative politics. We need to start thinking about it" ("Adam Przeworski: Capitalism, Democracy, and Science" 2003).

2. Domestic institutions can help mitigate competition among elites, which we discuss in more detail in Chapter 2.

3. Though leaders in authoritarian regimes need the support of a certain number of individuals in order to stay in power, they do not need the backing of each and every member of the elite. Most elite citizens support the dictator, but there may be some who do not. The exact number of elites required to keep the dictator in power is unknown and varies from regime to regime.

4. Though this study emphasizes elite politics, governance by a political party or professionalized military affects more than just elite-leader relations. It also impacts the nature of most other regime institutions, such as electoral, legislative, and security.

5. For more information on these categorizations, see Geddes 2003.

6. According to Paul Brooker (2000), modern authoritarianism differs substantially from earlier forms of authoritarian rule in that monarchs and chiefs are no longer the primary individuals in power. Amos Perlmutter (1981) points out that modern authoritarianism depends on the existence of political elites, popular support, political mobilization, and specialized political structures and institutions.

7. See Haber 2006 and Magaloni 2008 for a further critique of this theory. For a discussion of the quantitative methods used in the test of this theory, see Clarke and Stone 2008; the authors find that when the appropriate methods are implemented, the results fail to support the predictions of the theory.

8. See Geddes 2004 for an in-depth analysis of the personalization of dictatorships and regime consolidation.

9. Though we assume that all leaders try to maximize power, this is not to say that all factions within the regime share the same goal. As multiple studies have shown, elites in military dictatorships often *choose* to leave power as a result of factional infighting (Finer 1975; Bienen 1978; Decalo 1976; Kennedy 1974; Van Doorn 1968).

10. The most central features of autocracies rarely change after the first three years in power (Geddes 2003).

11. The institutional fluidity of authoritarian regimes will lead to endogeneity problems and measurement error in nearly *all* empirical tests examining the relationship between authoritarian domestic institutions and domestic and international political outcomes. We address the problem of endogeneity in more detail in Chapter 2 and take it into account in our statistical tests. The problem of measurement error is a more difficult fix. Its effect should primarily be to make it harder for empirical tests to reveal systematic trends of behavior across institutionally based categorizations of dictatorship. Despite the likely presence of measurement error, the tests we present in this study consistently show a relationship between the authoritarian domestic institutions that we emphasize and a range of political outcomes, which should point to the strength of these relationships.

2
Leadership

In East Germany in 1967, discontent with Walter Ulbricht from within the Communist Party had begun to grow due to Ulbricht's eagerness to cooperate with the West in return for economic aid. Interestingly, the strongest criticisms of Ulbricht came from within the Politburo, in the form of a faction led by his former protégé Erich Honecker, who seized upon elite dissatisfaction with Ulbricht's policies in the Politburo and assembled a group of supporters to oppose him. This group included Willi Stoph (chairman of the Council of Ministers), Hermann Axen (Ulbricht's foreign affairs specialist), and Gunter Mittag (Ulbricht's economic affairs specialist). Even though the creation of an opposition faction was considered a grievous party crime, Honecker managed to garner sufficient support for his faction by running a convincing underground campaign. Ulbricht's removal was smooth and devoid of violence. He officially retired due to "poor health" on May 3, 1971. Honecker quickly took over and Ulbricht was given the ceremonial position of chairman of the Council of State (Sarotte 2001; Grieder 2000; McAdams 1985).

Speculations about how long dictators will stay in power often appear in news editorials and headlines. Ranging from past predictions of the fates of Fidel Castro and Saddam Hussein, to current discussions of the fortunes of Hugo Chávez and Robert Mugabe, the rise and fall of dictators has long captured the attention of casual political observers, government intelligence agencies, and foreign policy analysts alike. Despite the world's fascination with dictators, the causes of leadership survival in dictatorships remain largely unidentified. Some dictators seem to rule forever, while others are easily overthrown. As Giacomo Chiozza and Henk Goemans point out, "very little is empirically known about the factors that affect the tenure of leaders" (2004, p. 604).

A number of studies have addressed specific types of leadership change. There are, for example, multiple studies that address the underlying causes of military coups in developing countries, a subset of the world that has seen its fair share of dictatorships (Jackman 1978; O'Kane 1989; Johnson, Slater, and McGowan 1984).[1] A central finding in this literature is that poverty is a good predictor of coups (Londregan and Poole 1990). Only a handful of scholars, however, have empirically addressed the likelihood of coups in which leadership turnover occurs but not necessarily regime change. Henry Bienen and Nicolas van de Walle (1991) find that leadership turnover is inversely related to the length of time a leader is in office. By the second decade leaders are in power, the risk they face of being ousted is half that of the first decade. In a similarly influential study, John Londregan and Keith Poole (1990) find, among other things, that coups are more likely to occur following recent coups. Economic conditions are also shown to affect leadership tenure in dictatorships. Because the leader's support group values a strong economy and the personal profits that accompany it, the dictator's survival is more likely as productivity and investment increase (Gallego and Pitchik 2004). The way in which power is assumed is posited to influence the risk of ouster as well. African leaders who assume power via extralegal means are more likely to be deposed than leaders who are legally chosen (Bienen and van de Walle 1989). Last, there is some evidence that personality and charisma influence the survival of dictators (Bratton and van de Walle 1997; Jackson and Rosberg 1982).

Largely missing from this literature, however, is an analysis of how the institutional structure of regimes affects the survival of the dictator. Though there is evidence that dictators face a lower risk of ouster in any given year than democrats (Bienen and van de Walle 1991; Bueno de Mesquita et al. 2003), few studies have addressed how differences in the internal makeup of dictatorships affect the tenure of autocratic leaders (for exceptions to this, see Gandhi and Przeworski 2007 and Bueno de Mesquita et al. 2003).[2]

In this chapter, we examine how institutional differences across dictatorships influence the survival of the leaders who rule them. Our argument emphasizes the role of elites. Elite responsibility for the downfall of dictators often runs counter to conventional perceptions about how dictatorships work. The assumption that mass revolutions, external interventions, revolts by dissatisfied groups, or military coups led by junior officers are the primary means by which dictators are overthrown still pervades the discourse of academic and policy circles alike.[3] This assumption persists despite the fact that individuals who are not members of the elite—whether civilian or military—are infrequently at the helm of successful coups (or other efforts) that prompt dictators to leave power. The importance of the dictator's elite supporters, often highlighted in scholarship on regime transitions (see Higley and Burton 1989; Kugler and Feng 1999; Haggard and Kaufman 1995), has only recently surfaced in research on the survival of dictators (Svolik 2009; Gallego and Pitchik 2004; Gandhi and Przeworski 2007).

We identify two key dimensions that shape the nature of leader-elite relations in dictatorships. These dimensions, taken together, influence the capacity of elites to oust dictators. The first dimension is whether elites share membership in a unifying institution. Membership in a dominant party or military, as in single-party and military dictatorships, makes it easier for elites to coordinate to overthrow the leader. The second dimension is whether elites have control over the security forces, as in military regimes. Direct influence over the security apparatus makes it easier to stage a coup. It follows that elites in military regimes should have the greatest ability to overthrow the dictator, followed by elites in single-party regimes, and lastly elites in personalist regimes.[4]

We stress that the downfall of dictators is often distinct from the downfall of dictatorships. These two are not one and the same. This distinction cannot be overstated. Authoritarian regimes frequently last well beyond the ouster of any individual leader.[5] We focus on the group that leaders rely on for support, rather than the group that regimes rely on for support. Conflation of these two groups can lead to misunderstandings of the causes of both regime change and leadership change. Our argument examines the factors underlying how leaders, not regimes, fall from power.

We test multiple implications of our argument quantitatively. The data analysis shows that elites in military dictatorships are the most capable of ousting their own leaders. As a result, military dictators face the greatest risk of being overthrown in any given year. The ousters do not usually lead to regime change. The opposite is true of personalist dictatorships. Elites in personalist dictatorships have the greatest difficulty ousting dictators and, consequently, personalist dictators face the lowest risk of being removed from power in any given year. When they are ousted, their regimes usually collapse, taking many of their erstwhile allies down with them. In short, the institutional structure of the dictatorship strongly influences the domestic vulnerabilities that dictators face.

How Authoritarianism Affects the Ability of Elites to Oust Dictators

By definition, dictatorship means that rulers wield extraordinary power. Other domestic actors have political influence to the extent that they can credibly threaten to remove the dictator from power. Since most dictators are ousted by members of their own inner circle, those who can credibly threaten ouster are usually the dictator's closest allies.

We argue that the presence of military or party organizations in government influences the ability of elites to topple dictators. We emphasize the ability of elites to forcibly remove leaders from power, as the threat of a coup carries greater weight than the threat of impeachment. This does not mean that the use of force is always necessary to unseat dictators. In the military dictatorship of Uruguay, for example, frustrated with President Juan María Bordaberry's inability to adequately deal with the country's economic troubles, elites demanded that he resign in 1976. Bordaberry acquiesced to their demand and power was peacefully transferred (Klieman 1980). Dictators heed orders to leave office when a credible threat of forcible removal backs these orders.

Membership in a Unifying Institution

The first dimension we highlight is whether members of the support coalition share membership in a unifying institution. Membership in a unifying institution enables elites to bargain with the dictator as a collective rather than as individuals who can easily be replaced by others (Geddes 2004). Professionalized militaries and parties tend to be unifying institutions. They are largely self-enforcing bargains, in that membership provides elites with benefits that they are willing to fight for if infringed upon (Brownlee 2008; Reuter and Remington 2009; Anugwom 2001; Feaver 1999).[6] The desire to preserve these benefits creates shared interests among the elite.[7] Membership in the military or party fosters elite unity, making it easier for elites to bargain with the dictator collectively.[8] In this way, the behavior of elites embedded in military hierarchies or single-party organizations is analogous to that of workers in a union. A union has more bargaining power than do individual workers, since the threat to strike is more potent than the threat to quit (Mulvey 1978). Just as unionization increases the bargaining power of workers relative to employers, membership in a professionalized military or party increases the bargaining power of elites relative to leaders.

As a result, the power structures of military and single-party dictatorships are less tilted in the favor of leaders than they are in personalist regimes. In China, for example, regime leader Deng Xiaoping was said to be "less dominant inside the party councils than he was made to appear to the general public" (Unger and Dittmer 2002, p. 173). Prior to this, under Mao Zedong, "opposition to the emergence of a strong leader was shown by the resistance of other leaders to the accretion of power in Mao's hands" (Nathan 1973, p. 54). In fact, elites in single-party and military regimes are often powerful enough to implement provisions for leadership turnover. Argentina provides a good example of this. Prior to the coup that ousted the Peronist government, members of the military junta agreed to a ruling formula in which the presidency was rotated and power dispersed among the services in order to guard against any individual acquiring too much power (Remmer 1991, p. 39). Argentine coup-plotters agreed to the following stipulations: "Service rivalry must be minimized and there must be no *caudillos*—no military chief would be allowed to try to convert himself into a popular political leader. . . . The chiefs agreed that the commanders' junta—they themselves—would serve as the source of state power. Jobs and authority would be divided in three so that no service would predominate" (Gugliotta 1986, p. 1). Mexico offers another example of "term limits" in a dictatorship. Under the Institutional Revolutionary Party (PRI), leaders were forced to adhere to a strict six-year term, or *sexenio*. Provisions such as these reflect the greater bargaining power of elites relative to the dictator in military and single-party regimes.

Just as union membership makes it easier for workers to coordinate to stage a strike, common membership in a unifying institution makes coordination among members of the coalition less difficult. Elite coordination is necessary because no one can seize power alone;[9] most coups involve coordination costs. Indeed, coordination is central to the staging of a successful coup. The ousting of Soviet premier Nikita Khrushchev in 1964 provides a good illustration of this: "[The coup] was not carried out until its planners were certain that they had secured the cooperation of the KGB Majorities in the Central Committee and Presidium, and officials spanning the territorial party apparatus" (Gandhi and Przeworski 2007, p. 1282). Because elites in single-party and military dictatorship share membership in the party and military, respectively, it is easier for them to overcome coordination barriers.

In addition, just as employers facing a unionized work force have less autonomy in dismissals, leaders in military and single-party regimes have less control over membership in the elite coalition than personalist leaders do. This reduces the ability of single-party and military dictators to select to the coalition only those individuals unlikely to oust them. Leaders may try to influence membership in the coalition via promotions and forced retirements in the military or within the party, but they do not usually have full control of either recruitment or promotion. In China, for example, Mao could not exclude opponents or their views from the party (Nathan 1973, p. 59). Decades later, though Jiang Zemin was successful in appointing a few associates to the Standing Committee, he was not strong enough to ensure that other close associates fared well in elections at the Congress, suggesting that his influence was limited (Cheng and White 2003, p. 554). Similarly, in Malaysia, some of the closest associates of regime leader Mahathir Mohamad were defeated in the 1996 elections (Case 1997, p. 403). Top United Malays National Organization (UMNO) posts were decided in electoral fights rather than simply being assigned by the leader (Case 1994, p. 921).[10] In Singapore, as well, though regime leader Lee Kuan Yew stated that he preferred Tony Tan as prime minister, he had to "go along with the decision of younger ministers, who chose Goh [Chok Tong] instead" (Mutalib 2000, p. 329).

Leaders in military and single-party regimes have few other pools from which to draw elites apart from the military or the party. In the military dictatorship of Mali, for example, only a small number of officers were in the group of potential junta members (Bennett 1975, p. 251). Single-party and military dictators may try to create new pools by purging the party and bringing new members into its ruling body or creating paramilitary forces loyal to them personally, but these efforts are not always successful due to resistance from elites.[11] In single-party dictatorships, the party organization makes an effort to ensure that the party is the "exclusive route to membership of the ministerial elite and the more senior positions within the state" (Costa Pinto 2002, p. 452). Similarly, in military dictatorships, the military organization tries to control access to top positions in the officer corps.[12]

Membership in a unifying institution enables military and party elites to bargain with the dictator as a collective. There are two primary consequences of the unionlike collective bargaining of elites in military and single-party dictatorships: (1) elites face lower coordination costs when it comes to ousting the leader, and (2) leaders have less control over the selection of individuals who will comprise the coalition.

In contrast, in personalist dictatorships there is no institution that effectively unites elites. Parties and militaries exist, but they do not control their own promotions and they tend to be rife with factions, often based on ethnicity. Elites must overcome a greater coordination barrier in order to unseat the leader because they are not organized into a self-enforcing structure. Efforts to topple Idriss Déby of Chad, for example, were said to have failed due to lack of elite unity ("Chad: Coup Attempt Foiled, Government Says" 2006). In personalist dictatorships, the system is structured by politicians, rather than by institutions (Bratton and van de Walle 1997, p. 62; Acemoglu, Robinson, and Verdier 2004, p. 167). As a result, dictators have more bargaining power relative to elites in personalist regimes than in military or single-party regimes. As demonstrated in Belarus, by early 1995 Alexander Lukashenko had "established personal control over the entire state administration, the economy, and the media"; by 2001, his control grew to the "state bureaucracy, the security apparatus, and the electoral process itself" (Silitski 2005, pp. 86–87).

Personalist leaders also have more control over the selection of individuals who will comprise the coalition because they do not face a unionized support market. They can select individuals without the constraints of military or party guidelines for promotions. In Portugal under António Salazar, the composition of his elite support group reflected "the reduced presence of the truly political institutions of the regime as a central element for access to the government" (Costa Pinto 2002, p. 436). Instead, individuals in personalist dictatorships compete with one another to secure their spot in the coalition. If they choose, personalist leaders can select low-skilled individuals who are less likely to successfully unseat them.[13] As a result, personalist dictators' support groups typically comprise associates, friends, and family members of the dictator. The Philippines under Ferdinand Marcos provides a good example of this. Marcos's narrow base of support included former classmates and relatives. The primary quality needed to acquire a position was loyalty (Celoza 1997, p. 96). In fact, Marcos often awarded key positions in the business sector to his most loyal associates; no entrepreneurial skills were necessary (Celoza 1997). The same was true of Rafael Trujillo in the Dominican Republic, where 153 of Trujillo's relatives were employed by the government (Wiarda 1968, p. 74). Family members held the presidency, senatorial posts, and diplomatic assignments, as well as the position of commander in chief of the armed forces (Acemoglu, Robinson, and Verdier 2004, p. 173).

Personalist dictators also ensure that no individuals become too powerful through frequent rotations and purges. Saddam Hussein, for example, was notoriously suspicious of his aides and brutal toward those deemed disloyal. As Jerrold Post wrote:

> In 1979, when he fully assumed the reins of Iraqi leadership, one of his first acts was to meet with his senior officials, some 200 in number, of which there were 21 officials whose loyalty he questioned. The dramatic meeting of his senior officials in which the 21 "traitors" were identified while Saddam watched, luxuriantly smoking a Cuban cigar, has been captured on film. After the "forced confessions" by a "plotter" whose family had been arrested, the remaining senior officials were complimented for their loyalty by Saddam and were rewarded by being directed to form the execution squads. (1991, p. 6)

The Central African Republic's Jean-Bédel Bokassa was no better. Bokassa had no qualms about killing rivals nor their friends and family (Titley 1997, p. 43). In Zaire, as well, many of Mobutu Sese Seko's ministers were hanged in front of large audiences, such as his defense minister, Jerome Anany, his finance minister, Emmanuel Bamba, and his energy minister, Alexandre Mahamba, along with the former prime minister, Evariste Kimba (Schatzberg 1988, p. 81).

Because personalist dictators do not bargain with an institutionalized elite collective, they are often able to implement divide and conquer strategies to deter the emergence of potential rivals.[14] Zaire under Mobutu provides an excellent example of this. Mobutu created an environment "in which any person or group could be rewarded or punished selectively" (Acemoglu, Robinson, and Verdier 2004, p. 169). This was compounded by the fact that a multitude of Zairians were waiting anxiously to take their place. Mobutu liked to play "musical chairs" with elites and regularly transferred them in and out of office (Snyder 1992, p. 392; Turner 1988, p. 215).[15] The frequent rotation of posts served to maintain an aura of uncertainty and vulnerability (Leslie 1987, p. 70). As David Gould wrote: "the frequent cabinet shuffles and transfers of officials from region to region may be explained as largely reflections of the president's skill at using people while they can provide assistance to him and at the same time keeping factions separated from each other, thus preventing autonomous power centers from developing" (1980, p. 83). The career of Nguza Karl-i-bond is illustrative of Mobutu's tactics. Karl-i-bond joined Mobutu's circle in the 1970s and later became foreign minister; in 1977 he was accused of treason and sentenced to death; in 1979 he was pardoned and given the post of prime minister; in 1981 he was exiled, but by 1985 had returned to Zaire to become ambassador to the United States (Acemoglu, Robinson, and Verdier 2004, p. 170).

Elites in personalist dictatorships do not share membership in a unifying institution, like a professionalized military or party, thus decreasing their bargaining power relative to the dictator and increasing coordination barriers. Because elites in single-party and military regimes bargain with the dictator as a collective unit, their ability to overthrow the leader should be greater than in personalist regimes.

Control over the Security Forces

The second dimension we highlight is the extent to which members of the elite coalition have control over the armed and security forces.[16] Most coups are executed by members of the military forces (Kebschull 1994). The more direct control that elites have over such forces, the more the leader's position is at risk. Though all countries have militaries and individuals who are capable of executing coups, elites in military dictatorships tend to have greater control over the security forces than do elites in personalist and single-party regimes. In military dictatorships, most members of the elite coalition are military commanders of various forces. This puts elites in military dictatorships in "an excellent position for gaining support, both active and passive, from the required quotient of the armed forces" (O'Kane

1989, p. 335). Military elites have greater control over the troops and weaponry needed for ouster, and the armed forces tend to be at least partially controlled by members of the elite coalition rather than by the leader himself.[17] As a result, elites in military regimes usually have more resources and autonomy than do elites in single-party and personalist regimes. As Samuel Finer aptly put it: "The military possesses a vastly superior organization. And they possess arms" (1962, p. 5).

This is not the case in single-party and personalist dictatorships. Though members of the military are almost always part of the elite coalition in single-party and personalist regimes, they may not have direct control over troops and weaponry.[18] In Haiti under François Duvalier, for example, an attempted coup on June 28, 1958, failed because the plotters did not know that the arms had been moved from the army barracks to Duvalier's palace (Ferguson 1987, p. 41). In personalist dictatorships, leaders—who often come from the military themselves—typically command the armed forces and control the security apparatus.[19] Personalist dictators usually control military promotions, promote their cronies, and eliminate individuals whom they deem to be disloyal. In the Dominican Republic, for example, Trujillo controlled the army through a mixture of fear, patronage, and the frequent rotation of posts, inhibiting the development of strong personal followings within the military (Lopez-Calvo 2005). In the Central African Republic, Bokassa took this a step further: he held numerous military posts himself (Titley 1997, p. 44). Bokassa had total control over promotions and demotions in the army and used this power to weaken any potential threat from within the military. Personalist dictators also create paramilitary forces loyal to themselves to counterbalance any potential opposition to them from within the professional military. Duvalier deterred the threat of a military coup by fragmenting the armed forces and creating an alternative militia intended to serve as a counter to any potentially disloyal army force (Ferguson 1988, p. 39). This militia, known as the Militia of National Security Volunteers (MVSN), was made up of young males fiercely loyal to Duvalier whose purpose was "to blunt the power of the army" and provide Duvalier with information to detect subversion (Ferguson 1987, p. 40).

In single-party dictatorships, the military is subordinated to the party just as it is in democratic regimes. Soldiers are often immersed in party ideology through indoctrination campaigns and promoted according to party loyalty. In China under Mao, for example, the Red

Guard soldiers were forced to memorize long paragraphs of Mao's musings (Whitson 1969, p. 22). The loyalty of the People's Liberation Army (PLA) to the party was later demonstrated by its actions in the Tiananmen Square massacre of June 1989: having been indoctrinated in Communist Party ideology, PLA soldiers were hesitant to see the collapse of communist rule (Koh 2000, p. 27). In single-party dictatorships, party functionaries are embedded in the military to ensure its loyalty.

These differences should make the execution of a coup more difficult for elites in personalist and single-party regimes. Because elites in military regimes have greater access to and control over the forces that can potentially unseat the leader, the probability that military elites can successfully do so should be greater.

The two dimensions that we highlight—taken together—imply that military elites should have the greatest ability to oust dictators, followed by single-party elites, and lastly personalist elites. Our argument is summarized in Table 2.1.

Implications of the Argument

Because it is difficult to test our argument directly, we instead test its implications. The argument claims that (1) it should be more difficult for personalist elites to coordinate to overthrow the dictator than it is for military or single-party elites because personalist elites are not bound together by a unifying institution; and (2) it should be easier for military elites to overthrow the leader than it is for single-party or personalist elites because military elites have better access to the security and armed forces.

The first claim implies that personalist elites operate in a less institutionalized environment than do military or single-party elites.

Table 2.1 The Power of Elites

	Collective Actor?	Security Access?	Ability to Stage Successful Coup
Military elites	Yes	More likely	High
Single-party elites	Yes	Less likely	Medium
Personalist elites	No	Less likely	Low

This means that in personalist dictatorships there should be few institutionalized methods for regulating succession.[20] Whereas parties and militaries tend to have established guidelines for dictating promotions, such guidelines should be absent in personalist dictatorships. Elites from the inner circle should be less likely to succeed the dictator in personalist dictatorships than in military or single-party dictatorships. The lack of means by which to regulate succession should also make transfers of power more contentious and destabilizing in personalist dictatorships. The collapse of the regime should be more likely to occur following the removal of the dictator in personalist regimes than in single-party or military regimes (Geddes 2003).

1. Elites from within the ruler's support coalition should be less likely to succeed the dictator in personalist dictatorships than in military or single-party dictatorships.
2. Personalist regimes should be more likely to collapse if the dictator is ousted than military or single-party regimes.

With respect to the second claim, if it is true that military elites have greater control over the armed and security forces necessary to stage a coup than single-party or personalist elites, then coups should be more likely to occur in military regimes. The probability of a coup occurring in any given year should be greater in military dictatorships than in single-party or personalist dictatorships, all else equal.[21] The same should be true regarding the likelihood that a leader will be ousted via coup in any given year.[22] With greater access to troops and weaponry, the use of force as a means of settling disputes with leaders should be more frequent in military dictatorships.

3. The risk of a coup occurring in any given year should be greater in military dictatorships than in single-party or personalist dictatorships.
4. The risk that a leader will be overthrown in a coup in any given year should be greater in military dictatorships than in single-party or personalist dictatorships.

Last, if both of our claims are true, then it should be easier for military elites to oust dictators and more difficult for personalist elites. All else equal, leadership survival rates should be lowest in military dictatorships, followed by single-party dictatorships, and lastly personalist dictatorships.

5. Personalist dictators should face the lowest risk of being removed from power, and military dictators should face the greatest risk.

To test these implications, we use the ARCHIGOS dataset of Hein Goemans, Kristian Skrede Gleditsch, and Giacomo Chiozza (2007), which includes entry and exit dates of all leaders holding executive power for the 1919–1999 period. Leaders leaving office due to natural death are coded as censored observations (a similar approach is used in Bienen and van de Walle 1991; Bueno de Mesquita et al. 2003; and Marinov 2005). We omit instances in which multiple leaders held office during a single calendar year. In these cases, we keep a single country-year, which records (1) that a leadership change occurred, and (2) who the leader in power is at the start of the calendar year. The dummy variable, leadership failure, measures whether a leader was removed from power in a particular year. Formatting the data in this way is useful because data on most covariates are measured annually.[23]

In all of our tests, our primary causal variable is the authoritarian support coalition's ability to oust the dictator if they are dissatisfied with his performance. As a proxy for that, we use the classification of authoritarian regimes into military, single-party, and personalist using Barbara Geddes's (2003) dataset, which codes whether regimes are military, single-party, personalist, or hybrids of these three. Because we do not have theoretical expectations for how hybrid regimes should behave, we exclude these regimes from our sample in order to provide a clearer test of our argument. It is important to emphasize that including these regimes does not alter the basic results presented here or elsewhere in this study. Results from our tests including hybrids are available on request. Geddes codes regimes in existence since World War II lasting three years or longer. We create dummy variables for each regime type, noting the type of regime in power at the start of the calendar year. The total number of regimes included in our dataset is 133.

Given the natural institutional fluidity of dictatorships, discussed in Chapter 1, there will be some amount of measurement error in our proxy for authoritarian domestic institutions, as in nearly all others. Personalist phases, for example, often emerge within military and single-party regimes. Though such phases are not strong enough to constitute regime change, they are sizable enough to generate some level of error in the codings of regimes. In addition, the early days of most dictatorships are characterized by heightened institutional flux as the leader of the regime engages in efforts to consolidate power and personalize the regime (Geddes 2004; Haber 2006). The effect of this type of measurement error should primarily be to make it harder for patterns of behavior to emerge across institutionally based categorizations of dictatorship in empirical tests. Any empirical associations between these proxies and the political outcomes tested should point to the underlying strength of such relationships.

We include an array of economic and domestic political controls in our models to account for factors that could potentially be correlated with both regime type and leadership survival. All of these variables are lagged one year to reduce problems of endogeneity. To control for domestic economic conditions, we use gross domestic product (GDP) per capita (logged) and economic growth. Poor economic conditions have been shown to negatively affect leadership survival (Londregan and Poole 1990). Both of these variables are taken from the World Bank (2003). We also include a measure of the number of prior coups occurring in the prior six years, as coded by Goemans, Gleditsch, and Chiozza (2007). Studies have shown that past coups lead to future coups (Londregan and Poole 1990). In addition, we control for whether the country underwent a civil war, as measured by James Fearon and David Laitin (2003), and whether the state was involved in a militarized interstate dispute in which force was applied (using the Correlates of War–Militarized Interstate Dispute [COW-MID] dataset; see Jones, Bremer, and Singer 1996). Bruce Bueno de Mesquita and Randolph Siverson (1995) find that leaders who engage in war subject themselves to a domestic political hazard that threatens their retention of political power. Last, we account for the age of the leader, provided by Goemans, Gleditsch, and Chiozza's (2007) dataset, and for fuel exports (as a percentage of merchandise exports, logged), taken from the World Bank (2003), both of which have been shown to influence leadership survival (see Marinov 2005 and Bueno de Mesquita et al. 2003, respectively). Dummy variables measuring time period in five-year intervals and regions are included where noted.[24]

As is often the case, data for many of these variables are missing. Because the presence of missing data can potentially bias estimates and inferences, we use multiple imputation, specifically the techniques described by Gary King and colleagues (2001) with the EMis algorithm in *Amelia 2.1* (Honaker et al. 1999). Because there are almost no control variables for data prior to 1950, we are only able to include observations from 1950 to 1999. Five imputations were used for this dataset, which resulted in 2,175 observations in each of the five datasets. In the statistical analyses that follow, each model was estimated on each imputed dataset. The results were combined, accounting for variation within each dataset, as well as variation across the imputed datasets (Honaker et al. 1999).

Last, because it is likely that there are some unobservable factors that affect both the type of dictatorship and the dependent variable of interest, as Jennifer Gandhi (2003) has demonstrated, we present results from a Heckman selection model in every table (Heckman 1979).[25] This model controls for possible selection effects to ensure that the regime-type coefficients are not biased. To estimate the selection-corrected effects of authoritarian regime type, we use logged GDP per capita, civil war, region, fuel exports, and growth, all variables that are potentially correlated with particular types of dictatorships (Bueno de Mesquita et al. 2003; Geddes 2003, 2004; Bratton and van de Walle 1997). We generate multinomial logit estimates of the authoritarian regime type and use inverse Mills ratios generated from these predicted results in our models.[26]

Testing the Implications

First implication: Elites from within the ruler's support coalition should be less likely to succeed the dictator in personalist dictatorships than in military or single-party dictatorships. To test this implication, we restrict the sample to cases of leadership change, of which there are 171, and estimate the probability that a member of the preexisting support coalition will succeed the dictator using a logistic regression. We create a dummy variable, insider succession, which measures whether an elite member of the regime rules following the ouster of the dictator. Detailed information on the coding of this variable is included in Appendix A. The standard control variables mentioned previously are included, as well as a dummy variable measuring whether the regime has a legislature (as measured in Bueno de Mesquita et al. 2003) to account for the possibility that the presence of a legislature aids in the transfer of power from one member of the elite to the next. Because some countries have experienced multiple dictatorships, Huber-White robust standard errors are calculated to deal with the likelihood that regimes occurring within the same country are not independent from one another.[27] The results of this test are presented in Model 1 of Table 2.2.

Table 2.2 The Consequences of Ouster of the Dictator

Dependent Variable	Probability of Insider Succession (given ouster of the leader) Model 1	Probability of Regime Failure (given ouster of the leader) Model 2
Military dictatorship	17.89***	.02***
	(10.81)	(.02)
Single-party dictatorship	67.22***	.003***
	(59.67)	(.004)
Civil war	3.41	.02
	(11.24)	(.07)
Prior coups	1.34	.85
	(.38)	(.22)
Age of dictator	1.00	—
	(.02)	
Growth	39.92a	.05
	(129.07)	(.18)
GDP per capita (logged)	1.78	.18
	(3.16)	(.24)
Force	.44	2.14
	(.47)	(1.94)
Fuel exports (logged)	.37	1.92
	(.27)	(1.28)
Regime duration (logged)	—	1.69
		(.68)
Legislature	.38	—
	(.23)	
Number of observations	171	171
Number of countries	73	73
Pseudo R^2	.34	.39
Likelihood ratio test, coefficients of dictator dummy variables = 0		
χ^2	14.73	57.16
$(p > \chi^2)$	(.00)	(.00)

Notes: a. This coefficient is conspicuously large. As a robustness check, we also ran this model excluding growth. The results are virtually unchanged.

Estimation is by logistic regression from 5 multiply imputed datasets (King et al. 2001; Honaker et al. 1999); odds ratios are reported, with Huber-White standard errors (clustered by country) in parentheses. Each regression also includes dummy variables for region; Model 2 includes dummy variables for time. Coefficients on these (not reported) are available upon request. "—" indicates not applicable. * $p < .10$, ** $p < .05$, *** $p < .01$; two-tailed tests. Personalist dictatorship is the excluded category.

According to Model 1, the odds that regime insiders succeed the dictator are 17 times greater in military dictatorships than in personalist dictatorships and 67 times greater in single-party dictatorships than in personalist dictatorships. These are substantively large differences and are statistically significant at the .01 level or lower.

To assess whether the inclusion of the regime-type dummy variables significantly improves the ability of the model to predict the probability of insider succession given the ouster of the dictator, we use the likelihood ratio test (King 1989). This tests the ratio between the unrestricted model including the key independent variables of interest (i.e., military, single-party) and the restricted model excluding these variables.[28] The likelihood ratio test indicates that the null hypothesis (that the coefficients of the dictator dummy variables are jointly equal to 1) would be rejected (at the 1 percent level).[29]

These results support our expectations: regime insiders are less likely to succeed the dictator in personalist regimes than in single-party or military regimes.

Second implication: Personalist regimes should be more likely to collapse if the dictator is ousted than military or single-party regimes. To test this implication, we test the probability of regime collapse given the ouster of the dictator. We again restrict the sample to cases of leadership change and estimate the probability of regime failure using a logistic regression. We create a dummy variable, regime failure, which measures whether the regime collapsed in any particular year using Geddes's (2003) codings. All of the controls mentioned previously are included, with one exception: a measure of regime duration (logged) is substituted for age of the dictator in order to account for the possibility that the number of years a regime has been in power affects how long it will continue to be in power.[30] Huber-White robust standard errors are used. The results of this test are presented in Model 2.

The results indicate that, given the removal of the dictator from power, the odds of regime collapse in personalist dictatorships are 50 times ($.02^{-1} = 50$) as high as the odds of regime failure in military dictatorships, and 333 times as high as the odds of regime failure in single-party dictatorships. These are very large differences and are statistically significant at the .01 level. In addition, the likelihood ratio test indicates that the improvement in the likelihood obtained from including the regime-type dummy variables in the model is sufficiently large that it cannot be due to chance alone.

These results lend support to the second implication: personalist dictatorships are more likely to fall after the removal of the dictator than are military or single-party dictatorships. This indicates that it is difficult to deal with succession in regimes with weak institutions.

Third implication: The risk of a coup occurring in any given year should be greater in military dictatorships than in single-party or personalist dictatorships. We test this implication by looking at the effect of regime type on the risk of a coup occurring, taking into account the standard set of controls mentioned previously.[31] We measure coups using data from A. S. Banks (2001), who defines coups as extraconstitutional or forced changes in the top government elite or in the elite's effective control of the nation's power structure.[32] The estimation procedure we use is a Cox proportional hazard model. The Cox model estimates a "hazard rate" for the occurrence of a coup at a particular moment.[33] This hazard rate is modeled as a function of the baseline hazard (h_0) at time t, which is simply the hazard for an observation when all independent variable values are equal to 0, and a number of independent variables. Estimates of these covariates indicate proportional changes relative to this baseline hazard. A hazard ratio greater than 1 indicates an increase in the risk of a coup; a hazard ratio between 0 and 1 indicates a decrease in the risk of a coup.[34]

Though the Cox proportional hazard model is not based on any assumptions about the shape of the underlying survival distribution, the model does assume a multiplicative relationship between the underlying hazard function and the log-linear function of the covariates (an assumption of proportionality) (Fox 2002). In other words, it assumes that the ratio of the hazard functions for two observations with different values for independent variables does not depend on time. It is possible that this proportionality assumption does not hold, however, and that the impact of some of the covariates depends on time. Because of this possibility, we conduct an analysis of the scaled Schoenfeld residuals for the models that we estimate. All of the covariates meet the proportional hazard assumption. For this reason, we do not include interactions between our explanatory variables and the logarithm of time.[35]

In addition, we follow Chiozza and Goemans (2004, p. 607) and include a frailty term in our specification. A frailty term is an additional unmeasured covariate α_i that is sampled from a Gamma distribution with mean of 1 and variance of θ that multiplicatively affects the baseline hazard (see Therneau and Grambsch 2000, pp. 231–260).[36] It is similar to a random effect, in that it assesses whether some leaders are more likely to be ousted, all else equal. When α_i is greater than 1, the leader is more likely to lose power than would be expected, given the explanatory variables. When α_i is smaller than 1, the opposite is true. The frailty term essentially incorporates unmeasured heterogeneity across units. We cluster observations by countries, so that the frailty term is constant within country groups (Chiozza and Goemans 2004, p. 608). The idea is that some countries may have frailties that are systematically different from those of other countries, independent of the other covariates in the model. The results of the test of the third implication are presented in Model 3 of Table 2.3.

The results indicate that the risk of a coup is 82 percent lower $(1 - .18 = .82)$ in personalist dictatorships than in military dictatorships, and 89 percent lower in single-party dictatorships than in military dictatorships. These are substantively large differences. In addition, these effects are statistically significant at the .01 level, as is the likelihood ratio test statistic that tests the increase in likelihood obtained by including the dictator dummy variables.[37]

As predicted, the risk of a coup occurring is significantly greater in military dictatorships than in personalist or single-party dictatorships.

Fourth implication: The risk that a leader will be overthrown in a coup in any given year should be greater in military dictatorships than in single-party or personalist dictatorships. To test this implication, we create a dummy variable, failure by coup, which measures whether a coup occurred in which the leader was overthrown. Similar to the previous test, the estimation procedure we use is a Cox proportional hazard model; we include the standard control variables and a frailty term in the specification.

The results of this test are presented in Model 4. In comparison to military dictators, personalist dictators have an 82 percent lower risk of being overthrown in a coup and single-party dictators have a 90 percent lower risk of being overthrown in a coup. These differences are quite large. They are also statistically significant at the .01 level, as is the likelihood test statistic.

To check the robustness of these results, in Model 5 we exclude the first year of the leader's tenure from the sample, a period of

Table 2.3 The Risk of Coup

		Hazard of Failure by Coup		
Dependent Variable	Hazard of Coup: Model 3	Model 4	Model 5 (first year of leader's tenure excluded)	Hazard of Failure by Insider-Led Coup: Model 6
Personalist dictatorship	.18***	.18***	.14***	.18***
	(.08)	(.08)	(.07)	(.10)
Single-party dictatorship	.11***	.10***	.07***	.16***
	(.06)	(.05)	(.04)	(.11)
Civil war	1.72	1.41	1.23	1.02
	(.70)	(.61)	(.57)	(.58)
Prior coups	2.00***	1.98***	2.32***	2.01***
	(.32)	(.34)	(.47)	(.38)
Age of dictator	.94***	.94***	.93***	.94***
	(.01)	(.01)	(.01)	(.02)
Growth	.06	.02**	.02**	.79
	(.10)	(.03)	(.03)	(1.95)
GDP per capita (logged)	.71*	.76**	.68*	.76
	(.13)	(.15)	(.15)	(.18)
Force	.47*	.37*	.30**	.53
	(.21)	(.19)	(.17)	(.35)
Fuel exports (logged)	1.08	1.02	1.06	1.05
	(.17)	(.16)	(.18)	(.22)
Number of observations	2,175	2,175	1,937	2,175
Number of countries	83	83	83	83
Number of failures	70	64	58	36
Likelihood ratio test, coefficients of dictator dummy variables = 1				
χ^2	93.13	89.61	96.31	50.49
$(p > \chi^2)$	(.00)	(.00)	(.00)	(.00)
θ	1.02	1.03	1.30	1.45
Likelihood ratio test $\theta = 0$				
χ^2	15.63	13.04	17.04	8.30
$(p > \chi^2)$	(.00)	(.00)	(.00)	(.00)

Notes: Results of a Cox proportionate hazard model from 5 multiply imputed datasets (King et al. 2001; Honaker et al. 1999); hazard ratios are reported, with standard errors in parentheses. The frailty parameter θ measures the variance of a Gamma distribution with mean equal to 1. * $p < .10$, ** $p < .05$, *** $p < .01$; two-tailed tests. Military dictatorship is the excluded category.

heightened institutional fluidity during which coups often occur. The first year that leaders are in power is usually one of instability and may be driving the results. When these cases are excluded, the effects remain virtually the same.

Last, because it is possible that some of these coups are led by regime outsiders, we also test the risk of coup ouster by members of the ruling elite or their allies.[38] To do so, we create a new variable, ouster by insiders, which measures whether members of the dictator's support coalition or their allies are responsible for the removal of the dictator. Detailed information on how we coded this variable is included in Appendix A. We use this variable to construct another dummy variable, failure by insider-led coup, which measures when coup and ouster by insiders coincide. We test the risk of failure by insider-led coup in Model 6. Again, the effects are quite strong. Military dictators are at a much greater risk of being overthrown in a coup in a given year than are personalist or single-party dictators, even when the coup is explicitly carried out by elites or their allies.

Fifth implication: Personalist dictators should face the lowest risk of being removed from power, and military dictators should face the greatest risk. We test this implication by looking at leadership failure using a Cox proportional hazard model with a shared frailty term. This is one of the most general of the survival regression models because no assumptions are made regarding the nature or shape of the hazard function. It is important to note that predicting leadership turnover is distinct from predicting coups d'état. While coups often cause leadership turnover, leadership turnovers can occur without violence. Leaders may voluntarily step down from power in order to avoid a violent overthrow or for other reasons. The threat of a coup may be enough to induce a leader to leave office. For this reason, the dependent variable here is leadership removal, rather than coups. We include the same control variables as mentioned previously. The results of this test are presented in Model 7 of Table 2.4.

As Model 7 reveals, personalist dictators have the lowest likelihood of being overthrown and military dictators have the highest. In comparison to single-party dictators, personalist dictators are 58 percent less likely to be ousted and military dictators are 658 percent more likely to be ousted. These are substantively large differences and the effects are statistically significant at the .01 level, as is the likelihood ratio test statistic.

Table 2.4 The Risk of Ouster

Dependent Variable: Hazard of Leadership Failure	Model 7	Model 8	Model 9	Model 10	Model 11
		(excluding tenures in which leadership failure and regime failure coincide)			
Personalist dictatorship	.42***	.48**	.26***	.49*	.49*
	(.13)	(.17)	(.11)	(.17)	(.18)
Military dictatorship	7.58***	8.06***	2.56*	8.38***	8.84***
	(2.72)	(3.51)	(1.31)	(3.60)	(3.92)
Civil war	.93	.89	.72	1.00	.83
	(.29)	(.30)	(.27)	(.35)	(.30)
Prior coups	1.70***	1.81***	1.69***	1.88***	1.85***
	(.20)	(.24)	(.26)	(.25)	(.25)
Age of dictator	.96***	.96***	.97	.97***	.97***
	(.01)	(.01)	(.01)	(.01)	(.01)
Growth	.03***	.02***	.07**	.02***	.03***
	(.03)	(.03)	(.09)	(.03)	(.04)
GDP per capita (logged)	1.00	.93	.93	.91	.95
	(.13)	(.13)	(.14)	(.13)	(.13)
Force	.57*	.50*	.46**	.54*	.54*
	(.17)	(.18)	(.17)	(.19)	(.20)
Fuel exports (logged)	1.01	.93	.88	.94	.91
	(.09)	(.10)	(.10)	(.10)	(.09)
Size of selectorate	—	—	.38***	—	—
	—	—	(.07)	—	—
Size of winning coalition	—	—	.79	—	—
	—	—	(.15)	—	—
Freedom House score	—	—	—	1.01**	—
	—	—	—	(.01)	—
Polity score	—	—	—	—	1.11***
					(.02)
Number of observations	2,175	1,911	1,902	1,902	1,911
Number of countries	83	79	79	79	79
Number of failures	171	125	125	125	125
Likelihood ratio test, coefficients of dictator dummy variables = 1					
χ^2	102.03	75.88	55.66	72.85	72.07
$(p > \chi^2)$	(.00)	(.00)	(.00)	(.00)	(.00)
Θ	.59	.57	.69	.51	.62
Likelihood ratio test, $\theta = 0$					
χ^2	29.61	22.53	32.40	20.28	27.66
$(p > \chi^2)$	(.00)	(.00)	(.00)	(.00)	(.00)

Notes: Results of a Cox proportionate hazard model from 5 multiply imputed datasets (King et al. 2001; Honaker et al. 1999); hazard ratios are reported, with standard errors in parentheses. The frailty parameter θ measures the variance of a Gamma distribution with mean equal to 1. "—" indicates not applicable. * $p < .10$, ** $p < .05$, *** $p < .01$; two-tailed tests. Single-party dictatorship is the excluded category.

To ensure that the apparent fragility of military dictators is not caused by the fragility of military regimes (Geddes 2003), we also conduct tests excluding the tenures of dictators whose removal from office coincides with the collapse of the regime.[39] Model 8 reveals that the results change very little when these observations are excluded.[40] We exclude these observations in the robustness checks that follow in order to more clearly test our argument.

It may also be the case that elites are deterred from trying to unseat the dictator when they believe there is a possibility that doing so will precipitate a larger regime collapse and they will wind up out of power.[41] Though it is impossible to determine the motivations of elites in particular cases, we investigate this possibility by examining all of the cases in which dictators were ousted by insiders. Interestingly, we find that there are only six cases (out of 171) of the regime "accidentally" falling upon the leader's removal from power. We consider cases "accidental" when the evidence indicates that the ouster of the dictator unintentionally gave rise to the collapse of the regime. In five of the six cases, a member of the elite from the old regime remained in power following the regime's demise.[42] Only on one occasion (Chad in 1979) did elites remove the leader from power and wind up out of power themselves due to the fall of the regime.

We next test whether our results are robust to alternate classifications of dictatorships. In Model 9, we include in our specification a measurement of regime type, as used by Bueno de Mesquita and colleagues (2003), that focuses on the selectorate and the winning coalition. As discussed in Chapter 1, Bueno de Mesquita and colleagues argue that governments can be characterized by the size of the selectorate (the set of people who have a say in choosing leaders) and the size of the winning coalition (the minimum set of people whose support the incumbent needs in order to remain in power). Bueno de Mesquita and colleagues predict that it is easier for leaders to survive when the size of the winning coalition is small and the size of the selectorate is large.[43]

As Model 9 indicates, even when controlling for the selectorate and winning coalition variables, the effects of the dictator variables remain large, statistically significant at the .10 level or lower, and in the direction predicted. The hazard rate of a personalist dictator is 74 percent lower than the hazard rate of a single-party dictator, while the hazard rate of a military dictator is 156 percent higher than the hazard rate of a single-party dictator. Though the coefficient of the winning coalition variable is not statistically significant or in the direction expected, the coefficient of the selectorate variable is. As the size of the selectorate increases, the hazard rate a leader faces decreases, as Bueno de Mesquita and colleagues predict. Given that Bueno de Mesquita and colleagues essentially measure the selectorate variable by coding whether there is a legislature (see Bueno de Mesquita et al. 2003, p. 134), this result is also consistent with Jennifer Gandhi and Adam Przeworski's (2007) claim that the presence of a legislature lengthens the tenure of dictators.

We also control for two other measures of autocracy: Freedom House scores and Polity scores. Model 10 includes the average of Freedom House's (www.freedomhouse.org) annual measures of political rights and civil liberties, lagged one year and standardized to range from 0 to 100, with higher scores indicating greater freedom. The inclusion of this variable does not noticeably alter the coefficients of the dictator variables. The coefficient of the Freedom House variable is also statistically significant and indicates, interestingly, that the risk of being ousted increases by 1 percent as leaders bestow more political rights and civil liberties upon their populations, though the effect could be spurious.

In Model 11, we control for another measure of democracy, each regime's combined Polity score, using data from the Polity IV dataset (Polity IV Project 2007), which codes a state as autocratic or democratic using a 20-point scale. This variable ranges from +10 (strongly democratic) to −10 (strongly autocratic). The results show that the effects of the regime-type dummy variables remain the same. The Polity coefficient is also statistically significant and indicates, perhaps surprisingly, that a small increase in the state's Polity score, by 1 point, increases a leader's risk of being ousted by 11 percent. The robustness tests suggest that the measure of regime type that we use, as coded and identified by Geddes (2003), captures the institutions that shape elite politics.

Last, to ensure that elite-led leadership turnover is driving these results, we also test the risk of ouster by regime insiders (i.e., elites and their allies). Personalist dictators should face the lowest risk of removal by regime insiders, and military dictators should face the greatest risk. To do so, we use the ouster by insiders dummy variable mentioned previously. We use a Cox proportional hazard model with a shared frailty term, along with the standard controls, to estimate the

Table 2.5 The Risk of Ouster by Regime Insiders

Dependent Variable: Probability of Ouster by Insiders	Model 12	Model 13 (excluding tenures in which leadership failure and regime failure coincide)
Personalist dictatorship	.25***	.18***
	(.10)	(.08)
Military dictatorship	4.09***	5.96***
	(1.81)	(2.72)
Civil war	.70	.59
	(.27)	(.21)
Prior coups	1.89***	2.06***
	(.27)	(.30)
Age of dictator	.96**	.96**
	(.01)	(.01)
Growth	.46	.10
	(.73)	(.18)
GDP per capita (logged)	.90	.89
	(.14)	(.14)
Force	.89	.71
	(.31)	(.27)
Fuel exports (logged)	1.04	.98
	(.13)	(.12)
Number of observations	2,175	1,902
Number of countries	83	79
Number of failures	106	98
Likelihood ratio test, coefficients of *dictator dummy variables = 1*		
χ^2	91.01	104.74
$(p > \chi^2)$	(.00)	(.00)
Θ	1.19	.95
Likelihood ratio test, $\theta = 0$		
χ^2	32.41	21.00
$(p > \chi^2)$	(.00)	(.00)

Notes: Results of a Cox proportionate hazard model from 5 multiply imputed datasets (King et al. 2001; Honaker et al. 1999); hazard ratios are reported, with standard errors in parentheses. The frailty parameter θ measures the variance of a Gamma distribution with mean equal to 1. * $p < .10$, ** $p < .05$, *** $p < .01$; two-tailed tests. Single-party dictatorship is the excluded category.

hazard a leader faces of being removed from power by regime insiders. The results of this test are presented in Model 12 of Table 2.5.

The results show that the hazard rate of personalist dictators being overthrown by regime insiders is 75 percent lower than the hazard rate of single-party dictators, while the hazard rate of military dictators being overthrown by regime insiders is 308 percent greater than the hazard rate of single-party dictators. These effects are statistically significant at the .01 level, as is the likelihood test statistic. In Model 13, we also exclude tenures in which leadership failure and regime failure coincide. Doing so only increases the magnitude of the regime-type coefficients in the direction expected: personalist dictators face the lowest risk of being ousted by regime insiders, followed by single-party dictators, and lastly military dictators.[44]

*   *   *

Taken together, these tests of the five implications strongly corroborate our argument. Military leaders face the highest risk of being overthrown by their erstwhile supporters both because coalition members control arms and troops and also because the preexisting hierarchical organization of the military helps them overcome coordination problems. At the other extreme, personalist leaders, who select members of their coalition at will and try to select individuals who pose little threat to their continued rule, face few credible threats of overthrow. Their supporters, far from being organized into a preexisting structure that can help to overcome coordination problems, often compete with one another for the leader's favor. In single-party regimes, the party organization reduces the costs of coordination but does not give members of the elite coalition access to the physical means to overthrow the leader by force. These findings are remarkably robust and provide substantial evidence in support of our theoretical framework.

Conclusion

Unfavorable authoritarian leaders are often a central concern for foreign policy makers. Though many governments resort to military options as a solution for troublesome foreign dictators, such interventions are typically accompanied by significant costs. Thus it is important to understand the nuances of authoritarian regimes and the differences in vulnerabilities that authoritarian leaders face.

We have argued that the primary group responsible for the downfall of dictators is the dictator's elite support coalition, and have identified two key dimensions that jointly affect the elite coalition's ability to oust. The first dimension is whether elites share membership in a unifying institution. When elites share membership in a party or professionalized military organization, as in single-party and military dictatorships, it is easier for them to overcome the coordination barriers entailed in ousting the leader. Elites can more easily replace dictators without bringing about regime collapse than can atomized elite supporters. The second dimension is whether elites have control over the troops and weaponry required to stage a coup, as in military regimes. Greater access to and control over the security apparatus make it easier for elites to stage a coup. The expectation follows that elites in military regimes should have the greatest ability to overthrow the dictator, followed by elites in single-party regimes, and lastly elites in personalist regimes.

Testing five implications of our theoretical argument has yielded positive and remarkably robust results. Military dictators face the greatest risk of being overthrown in any given year and only rule on average for around three years. Their ousters usually do not lead to regime change. In military governments, coups are essentially "the institutionalized method for changing governments" (Kposowa and Jenkins 1993, p. 126). Personalist dictators, by contrast, face the lowest risk of being removed from power and rule on average for around ten years. When they are ousted, their regimes usually collapse, taking many of their erstwhile allies down with them. These results hold under a variety of circumstances, as well as when alternate measures of authoritarianism are accounted for. Taken together, the evidence provides strong support for our theoretical argument and the causal mechanisms that underlie it. Governance by a party or professionalized military institution affects the ease with which elites can credibly threaten to overthrow dictators and, in turn, the risks of overthrow that dictators face.

Our theoretical and empirical analyses reveal a rank ordering of leadership vulnerability across dictatorships. Leaders in military dictatorships are the most vulnerable to internal overthrow, followed by leaders in single-party dictatorships, and lastly leaders in personalist dictatorships. Hence, the domestic vulnerabilities that dictators face differ systematically across authoritarian regimes.

Our findings underscore the importance of the dictator's elite support group for understanding not only leadership survival in dictatorships, but also a range of other political outcomes. Indeed, political influence in authoritarian regimes comes from the ability to control the fate of the leader. Dictators heed those who can oust them. In this regard they are no different from democrats. Given that politicians care about getting and staying in office, elites should be seen as the dictator's primary constituent group. Dictators must factor in the preferences of their elites' constituents or risk removal from office. To understand what drives the decisions of dictators, we should look to the individuals whom dictators must please to stay in power: members of the elite coalition.

Notes

1. As we discuss later in this chapter, coup d'état is only one of many ways by which transfers of power occur in authoritarian regimes.
2. In Chapter 1, we briefly address theoretical issues with these studies. Here in Chapter 2, in its empirical portion, we also control for the key explanatory variables put forth in these studies.
3. This is not to say that such forms of ouster do not occur, but rather that they are rare in comparison to the proportion of elite-led leadership turnovers.
4. One might argue that it is not the military or the party that makes it possible for elites to overthrow the dictator, but rather that the dictator was not powerful enough to begin with to enable personalization of the regime. This argument, however, ignores the fact that the strength of party and military organizations prior to the seizure of power largely determines the capacity of leaders to personalize the regime (as discussed in Chapter 1). All leaders will seek personalization (i.e., maximization) of their power; the extent to which they will succeed in their efforts, however, depends on the preexisting organizational strength of their launching organizations (Geddes 2004; Haber 2006).
5. We follow Geddes and define regimes as "sets of formal and informal rules and procedures for selecting national leaders and policies" (2003, p. 16).
6. As a party official in the executive committee of United Russia in the Russian Federation stated, "If a member works for the benefit of the party, then it is in the party's interest to ensure that he sees some perspective in continuing to support the party" (Reuter and Remington 2009, p. 520).
7. We thank an anonymous reviewer for this insight.
8. Though military and party institutions help to unify elites, this does not mean that factions within them do not exist. On the contrary, elite fac-

tionalism is common in all types of dictatorship. In Barbara Geddes's (2003) game-theoretic models of authoritarian breakdowns in personalist, military, and single-party regimes, for example, competition among rival factions is a defining feature of all three. Institutions do not drive whether factions will exist, but rather provide structure for how factional competition will occur. In particular, Geddes shows that unique features of military rule make factional competition far more destabilizing to military regimes than to other forms of dictatorship. For a further discussion of how institutions shape factional politics in dictatorships, see Geddes 2003.

9. Assassinations can, of course, be carried out by a single individual. Without the backing of other elites, however, killing the leader does not ensure that one's power is secured.

10. As William Case writes, UMNO even allows "challenges to the top position holders so long as they are supported by two divisional nominations" (2002, p. 113).

11. When such strategies do work, they lead to personalization, "the concentration of decisionmaking and coercive power in the hands of one person, unfettered by a party central committee or institutionalized military decision-making process" (Geddes 2004, p. 13), and consequently to change in regime type.

12. Though civilians often hold political positions in military dictatorships, power ultimately rests with the military elite (Bienen 1978, p. 221).

13. As Paul Lewis points out, personalist dictators choose to shift subordinates in and out of office frequently, "so that no subleader gets too entrenched or builds up an independent power base" (1978, p. 622). In Middle Eastern personalist dictatorships, for example, elites "have predominantly consisted of those who were most closely and personally affiliated with the regime leadership. Loyalty [tends to be] the most indispensable quality needed . . . and political competence play[s] a secondary role" (Albrecht and Schlumberger 2004, p. 378).

14. Leaders in military and single-party regimes also engage in these strategies, though they tend to be less successful.

15. Blaine Harden lends more support to this: "Conventional wisdom in Kinshasa says that besides Mobutu and his family only 80 people in the country count. At any one time, 20 of them are ministers, 20 are exiles, 20 are in jail and 20 are ambassadors. Every three months, the music stops and Mobutu forces everyone to change chairs" (1987, p. A1).

16. In those regimes in which paramilitary forces exist, we assume that individual elites are not directly in charge of them.

17. Lower-level members of the military, such as junior officers, also have access to the means by which to stage a coup. Junior officer–led coups, however, are less likely to be successful given that they lack the support of military elites. In such scenarios, officers must not only mobilize their peers, but also do so without alerting the suspicions of members of the military elite or those loyal to them.

18. In addition, though it is fairly common for some elites in personalist and single-party dictatorships to be current or former members of the mili-

tary, in military dictatorships it is impossible to obtain elite status without current membership in the military.

19. This was true of Gambia's Yahya Jammeh, Ghana's Jerry Rawlings, Guinea's Lansana Conté, Libya's Muammar Qaddafi, Madagascar's Didier Ratsiraka, and Venezuela's Hugo Chávez, to name a few.

20. In China, for example, the leadership stressed the need for "institutionalized succession" (Cheng and White 2003, p. 556). As Lowell Dittmer writes, "Owing perhaps to a political tradition of dynastic succession in the absence of primogeniture, the Chinese leadership has invested a great deal of political capital in the preliminary making and recurrent reconsideration of anticipatory succession arrangements" (2003, p. 913). In Tanzania, as well, the ruling Tanganyika African National Union (TANU) "managed the transition from power of its founding president, Julius Nyeyere, with little difficulty in 1985" (Smith 2005, p. 428).

21. In other words, assuming equal elite grievances with the dictator (which a number of control variables in our tests are intended to proxy for), it should be easier for military elites to stage a coup and more difficult for personalist elites. Just because elites are capable of staging a coup does not necessarily mean that they will do so, absent reason or desire to carry out such an effort.

22. Coups do not always lead to permanent leadership turnover. Leaders occasionally regain power immediately following a coup.

23. John Londregan and Keith Poole (1996) use a similar approach.

24. We use regional dummy variables rather than fixed effects so that countries in which only one dictator has ruled are not dropped from the analysis. Regions include Africa, Asia, Eastern Europe, Latin America, and the Middle East and North Africa.

25. Personalist dictatorship, for example, by definition implies that the leader was victorious in the power struggle with elites following the seizure of power. This presents a selection issue for studies investigating how personalism influences leadership survival.

26. Consistent with other similar studies, we do not include in any of our tables the estimates of the inverse Mills ratios obtained from the multinomial logit model predicting regime type. It is beyond the scope of this study to examine in detail the meaning of the selection effects. Their interpretation is complex and highly dependent on model specification (see Dolton and Makepeace 1987).

27. Huber-White standard errors were generated by using the "cluster" option in STATA 9 to group regimes within the same country. Huber-White standard errors adjust for correlations of error terms across observations (Huber 1967).

28. Because the likelihood ratio test statistic cannot be computed with clustered standard errors, clustered standard errors are not used when computing the statistic.

29. We test whether the coefficients are jointly equal to 1, as opposed to 0, because odds ratios are used instead of logits.

30. Because age and regime duration are highly collinear, both variables cannot be included simultaneously in the model.

31. This implication looks at the ability of elites to stage successful coups. We do not include here a test of the likelihood of attempted coups because our argument does not generate clear expectations about when coups will fail. It may be that coups are more likely to fail in personalist and single-party regimes, because elite actors are less likely to have military training (or access to highly trained military personnel). But the converse could also be true, in that coups staged by party and personalist elites may be less likely to fail because elites are less likely to stage them in the first place unless they are bound to be successful.

32. Banks's measure captures irregular transfers of power, such that a palace coup in a single-party dictatorship carried out by one faction against another is considered a coup. Using such an inclusive measure of coups should only make it more difficult for our tests here to generate the expected results.

33. The hazard rate is defined as:

$$h(t) = \frac{\text{probability of leadership removal between times } t \text{ and } t + 1}{\text{probability of leadership removal after time } t}$$

34. A hazard ratio of .75, for example, would indicate 25 percent lower $(1 - .75)$ risk, while a hazard ratio of 1.25 would indicate 25 percent greater $(1.25 - 1)$ risk.

35. Graphs of the residuals and time also do not indicate nonproportionality.

36. The specification for the hazard takes the following form:

$$h_i\,(t \mid \mathrm{x}) = h_{0i}(t)\alpha_i \exp\left(\Sigma_{j=1}^{p}\beta_j\,x_j\right)$$

where $h_{0i}(t)$ is the baseline hazard, and α_i follows a Gamma distribution with shape and scale parameters equal to $1/\theta$.

37. The likelihood ratio tests whether the coefficients are jointly equal to 1, as opposed to 0, because the coefficients reflect hazard ratios.

38. Elites may enlist their allies in the security forces or military to actually carry out the coup.

39. In this sample, tenures are excluded if leaders were removed from office during the last year of the regime. Because leadership removal and regime collapse nearly always coincide in personalist regimes, we do not exclude any personalist tenures. Doing so does not alter the results.

40. The results also hold in tests in which the first year of the leader's tenure—a potentially unstable period—is removed from the sample. In addition, though term limits are rare, they have been used in some dictatorships, notably regimes in Brazil, El Salvador, Mexico, Uruguay, and Yugoslavia. Excluding these regimes from the sample does not alter the results, which can be obtained upon request.

41. It is often the case, particularly in military regimes, that elites remove the leader from power with the intention of leaving power themselves in the near future. These cases would not be considered accidental regime collapse.

42. The possibility of the regime collapsing is probably not of concern to elites if they are likely to remain in power.

43. Our results remain even when an alternate measure from Bueno de Mesquita and colleagues (2003), the ratio of winning coalition to selectorate, is included.

44. The results hold in tests in which the first year of the leader's tenure is removed from the sample, as well as when other classifications of dictatorship are included.

3
Conflict Behavior

W hy states choose to escalate conflicts with other states is one of the fundamental questions of international relations. Much of the dialogue addressing this question has focused on the lack of perfect information between states: crises escalate because states have uncertainty regarding the intentions of their adversaries (Herz 1950; Jervis 1978; Waltz 1959). If all states perfectly knew the objectives of other states, there would be no conflict. International crises occur "precisely because state leaders cannot anticipate the outcome, owing to the fact that adversaries have private information about their willingness to fight over foreign policy interests and the incentive to misrepresent it" (Fearon 1994, p. 583). Conflicts are avoided when states are able to signal to their adversaries that they mean business, that their threats are more than just "cheap talk."

Some states are better able than others to signal that their threats are credible. A key factor that enables states to convey such signals is the presence of domestic institutions. Conflicts between democracies rarely occur, for example, because democracies possess institutions that better enable them to signal resolve (Schultz 1998; Siegel 1997).

In democracies, when leaders make public threats, and then back down, their domestic audiences—voters—punish them for having done so (Fearon 1994).[1] By going public with their demands, leaders establish a hands-tying mechanism, creating audience costs that they would suffer if they fail to follow through with their threats (Fearon 1994, 1997; Schultz 1998, 2001; Ramsay 2004; Smith 1998). The logic is that domestic audiences see threats and the deployment of troops as "engaging the national honor" of the state (Fearon 1994).[2] Indeed, using experiments embedded in public opinion surveys, Michael Tomz (2007) shows that these audience costs arise primarily because citizens care about the international reputation of the country or leader. Democratic leaders are better able to signal their commitment during crises than dictators are because they face high domestic costs for backing down on their threats, causing their adversaries to take them seriously (Fearon 1994). Multiple studies present evidence consistent with this claim (Eyerman and Hart 1996; Schultz 1999; Partell and Palmer 1999; Gelpi and Griesdorf 2001).

Dictatorships, however, are not a uniform group. Lumping them together may conceal important variations in the ability of dictators to establish hands-tying mechanisms and credibly signal their resolve (Prins 2003; Weeks 2008).[3] In recent years, international relations scholars have begun to unpack the category "nondemocratic." Though this literature is relatively limited, disaggregating dictatorships into multiple groups has proved fruitful, revealing interesting patterns of behavior. One study has found, for example, that no two personalist dictatorships or two military dictatorships have ever gone to war with each other since 1945 (Peceny, Beer, and Sanchez-Terry 2002). In addition, single-party dictatorships are less likely to be targets of military disputes than are other forms of dictatorship (Peceny and Butler 2004), while military regimes are more likely than single-party regimes to initiate military disputes, irrespective of whether those regimes are highly personalized (Lai and Slater 2006). There is also some evidence that personalist dictatorships fight wars poorly (Reiter and Stam 2003) and face signaling disadvantages during disputes (Weeks 2008).

In this chapter, we draw from this literature and examine the relationship between authoritarian political institutions and international conflict behavior. We show that differences in the makeup of dictatorships affect the capacity of dictators to send signals of resolve during interstate crises; some dictators are more capable than others of communicating their intentions and conveying the credibility of their threats. We argue that the ability of dictators to signal their resolve during conflicts depends on how easy it is for their domestic audiences to impose costs on them for backing down. In dictatorships, the domestic audience is the leader's elite support group. When it is easy for elites to unseat dictators, it is easy for the regime to generate audience costs and, consequently, for the leader to communicate his intentions.

Our argument builds on the work of Jessica Weeks (2008), who contends that coordination is key to unseating dictators: when domestic groups can coordinate to punish the leader, they can hold leaders accountable for their actions, enabling the regime to generate audience costs. We posit that in addition to coordination, control over troops and weaponry is also crucial. When domestic groups lack direct access to the forces necessary to punish the leader, low coordination barriers become less powerful.

As we show in Chapter 2, elites face the fewest difficulties deposing unfavorable leaders in military dictatorships and the most difficulties doing so in personalist dictatorships. Military leaders encounter the highest risk of being overthrown by their elite support group both because elites control arms and troops and also because the organizational structure of the military helps them overcome coordination problems. At the other end, personalist leaders, who have full control over membership to their support group and select individuals who pose little threat to their power, face few credible threats of overthrow. Their supporters, far from being organized into a unifying structure that can help to overcome coordination barriers, often compete with one another for the leader's approval. In single-party regimes, the party organization lowers coordination costs but does not give members of the elite coalition access to the physical means to force the leader out of power.

For these reasons, we expect that elites in military dictatorships should be best able to punish dictators for poor foreign policy choices, followed by elites in single-party dictatorships, and lastly elites in personalist dictatorships. Military dictators should be the most capable of generating high domestic costs for backing down on their threats and, as a result, should be better able to signal their resolve. The opposite should be true of personalist dictators.

The quantitative evidence we present in this chapter supports this expectation. Our findings suggest that among dictatorships, leaders in military regimes are best able to convey the credibility of their threats, followed by leaders in single-party regimes, and lastly leaders in personalist regimes.

How Authoritarianism Influences the Credibility of Dictators' Threats

The idea behind audience costs is that political leaders risk their careers when backing down because some "audience" has the capacity to oust them from office (Fearon 1994). Democratic leaders are better able to generate these domestic audience costs than their autocratic counterparts because it is easier for their domestic publics to punish them for backing down on their threats. In democracies, elections are the vehicles by which leaders are held accountable for their past actions. Democratic leaders risk their electoral futures by publicly making bold, threatening statements during international altercations: if they fail to follow through on their threats, they could be voted out of office. In authoritarian regimes this is not the case. Where there are no free and fair elections, there is no easy or routine way for citizens to pass judgment on the leadership. There is no mechanism by which the public can hold leaders accountable short of social revolution. When an authoritarian leader makes an outrageous public statement, there are few domestic political costs to pay for conceding at the last minute.[4] Because democratic leaders suffer greater domestic costs than authoritarian leaders when they make public threats and then back down on them, they are better able to communicate their intentions to foreign governments. James Fearon (1994) points out that this argument helps to explain the democratic peace: because democracies can more clearly signal their intentions, they are able to moderate the security dilemma between them. When there is complete information about resolve, there is no public crisis. The outcome can be seen in advance; the state that would ultimately be defeated backs down.

The personalist dictatorship of Libya under Muammar Qaddafi provides a good example of how this process plays out. Notorious for issuing bold threats,[5] Qaddafi has repeatedly meddled into the political affairs of his African and Middle Eastern neighbors and engaged in multiple careless foreign policy ventures. Even so, he has never been punished for this behavior at home. Because of this, Qaddafi's provocations are rarely viewed as credible by his adversaries. Rather than backing down when goaded by Qaddafi, enemy states often assume that he is bluffing and raise the stakes. In fact, Qaddafi's provocations have led to armed conflict with five of his six neighbors (Black 2000, p. 13; Viorst 1999). Because he historically has not suffered domestic consequences for issuing empty threats, Qaddafi's threats are typically seen as nothing more than "hot air" in the eyes of his adversaries. In 1973, for example, Qaddafi declared the Gulf of Sidra to be Libyan territorial waters and, in doing so, challenged the US naval presence in the eastern Mediterranean. In August 1981,

Qaddafi decided to further pester the United States and sent Libyan fighter planes to patrol the area. The United States quickly called Qaddafi's bluff shortly after and shot down two Libyan Su-22 jets. Rather than retaliate, Qaddafi chose not to follow through on his claims to the Gulf (Gunter 2001). Even though Qaddafi has repeatedly caved in on his stated foreign policy commitments, he remains in power, much to the chagrin of his neighbors. As Qaddafi's case exemplifies, when leaders face little accountability at home, they can go back on their word without facing domestic repercussions and, consequently, will encounter difficulties conveying to their enemies the credibility of their threats.

Of course, not all dictatorships are like Libya's under Qaddafi. Given the heterogeneity of dictatorships, it is highly likely that some dictators do face domestic costs for backing down on their stated commitments and, in turn, are capable of signaling their resolve during disputes. Indeed, Weeks (2008) shows that in most political regimes, domestic groups can hold leaders accountable for their actions, enabling the leaders to establish a hands-tying mechanism and generate audience costs. We build on Weeks's study and examine how dictatorships vary in this regard. We argue that key to understanding audience costs in dictatorships is identifying (1) which actors can impose costs on the dictator, and (2) the ease with which they can do so.

The Domestic Audience

Audience costs require that domestic groups can impose costs on leaders (i.e., remove them from power) for poor foreign policy choices.[6] To understand how dictatorships differ in this regard, it is first important to identify which domestic group has this capability. In democracies, this group is fairly easy to identify: the electorate. In dictatorships, however, it is far less obvious. Who can impose costs on a dictator? After all, "autocratic institutions eschew such notions as electoral competition and accountability to the populace, while democratic institutions generally embrace these ideals" (Kinne 2005, p. 119).

Despite the lack of transparent and institutionalized mechanisms for imposing costs on leaders in dictatorships, all dictators are politically accountable to some domestic audience (Kinne 2005, p. 120). In dictatorships, this audience is the dictator's elite support group. Leaders must stay in the good favor of elites or risk being overthrown (see Chapter 2). As Weeks writes, "Most authoritarian leaders require the support of domestic elites who act as audiences in much the same way as voting publics in democracies" (2008, p. 36). Just as voters can make democratic leaders pay for failing to follow through with their commitments, so can elites in authoritarian regimes.

The Ease of Ouster

We argue that what varies across regimes is not whether elites *can* impose costs on dictators, but the *ease* with which they can do so. The level of audience costs in authoritarian regimes should be a function of how easy it is for members of the dictator's support group to overthrow the leader. According to Weeks, "the crucial question in generating international credibility is whether the relevant domestic audience can and will coordinate to sanction the leader" (2008, p. 36).[7] Like Weeks, we argue that elite coordination is a key factor in determining the support group's ability to oust the dictator and hold him accountable. As we show in Chapter 2, however, elite control over the security forces is also critical. In addition to low coordination barriers, access to the troops and weaponry required to forcibly remove the leader from power is an essential component in determining how easy it will be for elites to oust dictators should they choose to.

In personalist dictatorships, elites score low on both of these factors, making it very difficult for them to overthrow the leader. In single-party dictatorships, though elites face low barriers of coordination, they do not control the security forces, giving them less access to the tools needed to force the leader out of power. In military dictatorships, by contrast, elites not only encounter low coordination barriers, but also have control over the security apparatus, making it much easier for them to unseat the leader. As Chapter 2 reveals, military elites have the greatest ability to oust dictators, followed by single-party elites, and lastly personalist elites.

It follows that, among dictatorships, military leaders should have the highest price to pay for reneging on their commitments; in other words, they should be the most capable of generating audience costs. In contrast, personalist dictators should have the lowest price to pay if they make public threats and back down on them; they should be the least capable of generating audience costs. Because military dictators face the greatest potential costs for reneging on their commitments, they should be the most capable of signaling their resolve during interstate conflicts, followed by single-party dictators, and lastly personalist dictators.[8]

Our expectations differ from those of Weeks in one key way. Because Weeks does not emphasize elite access to the security forces, she does not expect military dictatorships to have any signaling advantages over single-party dictatorships, as both are characterized by equally low barriers to elite coordination. If our argument is true, however, military dictatorships—due to easy elite access to troops and weaponry—should be better able to signal their intentions during disputes than single-party dictatorships.

Testing the Argument

We test our argument quantitatively using the Correlates of War–Militarized Interstate Dispute (COW-MID) dataset, which identifies the initiator and target of each militarized interstate dispute (Jones, Bremer, and Singer 1996). Militarized interstate disputes are conflicts in which one or more states threaten, display, or use force against one or more other states. The dataset identifies the initiating side (which state in the dyad took the first militarized action against the other state in the dyad) and the target side. The dataset also codes whether the initiating or target state, or both, sought some revision of the status quo. In most cases, states on the initiating side seek revisions. Cases are broken down into dispute dyads, with one or more states in each dyad representing the initiator and the others representing the target.

Due to the methodological difficulty of directly testing the ability of domestic audiences to punish leaders for backing down on their threats (see Schultz 2001 and Baum 2004a), we follow others in the field (Schultz 1999; Prins 2003; Weeks 2008) and look at whether target states choose to reciprocate initiators' challenges.[9] As Kenneth Schultz writes:

> If there is reason to believe that some variable correlates with high audience costs, then it should also correlate with the outcomes that high audience costs are hypothesized to produce, such as a lower rate of resistance, a lower rate of backing down, and so forth. These tests are not plagued by the same problems of partial observability because they do not require the researcher to observe the audience costs directly. Instead they can be used to make inferences about the latent distribution of audience costs through the relative frequency of observable outcomes. (2001, p. 54)

States in which leaders incur high domestic costs for backing down on threats should elicit lower rates of reciprocation from their targets. The reciprocation of a challenge indicates that the target state has opted to escalate the crisis, rather than avoid a military response. The decision to reciprocate is a reasonable sign that the target state does not believe the challenge to be genuine: the threat-maker would not have to bear high audience costs for backing down (Schultz 1999, p. 251). In fact, roughly 50 percent of militarized actions are reciprocated by the target state (Jones, Bremer, and Singer 1996). Though a lack of reciprocation does not indicate that targets did not respond to the initial threat, it does imply that they did not believe it to be in their interests to escalate the conflict militarily. A willingness to reciprocate, on the other hand, "suggests that the target considered a military response potentially worthwhile" (Schultz 1999, p. 251).

The COW-MID dataset provides data on the highest hostility level reached by each state involved in a dispute. When the participant took no militarized action, a hostility level of 0 is recorded. When the hostility level reached by the target state was greater than 0, this implies that it responded with a threat, display, or use of force. We set the dependent variable, reciprocation, equal to 1 when the target state responded with a threat, display, or use of force, and equal to 0 when the target state took no militarized action.[10]

In some disputes, new states joined the conflict once it had already escalated. The COW-MID dataset codes these states as nonoriginators. Because we are interested in the initial threat and response of the target, we include in our sample only those dispute dyads in which both states were originating participants. One potential problem, however, is that in some cases there were multiple originating participants on one or both sides of the dispute. This is problematic because the probability of reciprocation is likely correlated among target states in the same dispute and likely affected by their beliefs about the resolve of the leading state in the group of initiators rather than the independent resolve of every member separately. Including these dispute dyads in the sample will introduce nonindependent observations. Following Kenneth Schultz (1999), we use two different methods to address this problem. The first method is to use Huber-White standard errors, which take into account nonindependence among dyads. The second method is to run regressions using the subsample of militarized interstate disputes that involve only one originating state on each side, or bilateral disputes.

To measure the ability of the authoritarian elite coalition to oust the dictator, we again use Barbara Geddes's (2003) codings of dictatorship.[11] We also include democratic regimes in the sample as a baseline comparison. To measure democratic regimes, we use the Polity IV dataset (Polity IV Project 2007), which codes country years as autocratic or democratic using a 20-point scale. We count as democratic those states receiving a score of 7 or higher on this variable, a procedure typically used in the literature.[12] Because only regimes with more than 1 million inhabitants lasting three years or longer are included in Geddes's dataset, we do the same in our coding of democratic regimes: we code them as democratic if they have more than 1 million inhabitants and achieved scores above 7 for three consecutive years or more. To increase the clarity of our findings, as in Chapter 2, we only test differences between democratic regimes, personalist dictatorships, military dictatorships, and single-party dictatorships, leaving out those regimes coded by Geddes as hybrids and periods of flux between regimes.[13] Our sample includes 819 dyads from 1946 to 2000 in which both initiators and targets could be classified as one of those four regime types.

Using these codings, we create eight dummy variables measuring the regime type of the target state and initiating state in each dispute dyad: personalist target, personalist initiator, single-party target, single-party initiator, military target, military initiator, democratic target, and democratic initiator.[14]

The expectation is that target states should be least likely to reciprocate disputes when the initiating state is a democracy, followed by military dictatorship, single-party dictatorship, and lastly personalist dictatorship. In Table 3.1, we present statistics of the incidence of dispute reciprocation for each regime type.

The table reveals a number of interesting characteristics about the sample. The first is that the number of military regimes in the sample is relatively small. There are only 45 dyads involving military targets and only 69 dyads involving military initiators. As a result, it may be difficult to make inferences about the conflict behavior of military dictatorships. The table shows that when personalist dictatorships initiate a dispute, the action is reciprocated 49 percent of the time; when single-party and military regimes initiate a dispute, the action is reciprocated 44 percent of the time; and when democratic regimes initiate a dispute, the action is reciprocated 35 percent of the time. In addition, corresponding with democratic peace theory, dis-

Table 3.1   Dispute Reciprocation, Given Regime Type

	Personalist Target	Single-Party Target	Military Target	Democratic Target	Total
Personalist initiator	19 / 37	27 / 52	9 / 13	34 / 77	89 / 179
	(51%)	(52%)	(69%)	(44%)	(49%)
Single-party initiator	9 / 20	45 / 77	5 / 14	59 / 155	118 / 266
	(45%)	(58%)	(35%)	(38%)	(44%)
Military initiator	5 / 11	5 / 13	2 / 4	19 / 41	31 / 69
	(45%)	(38%)	(50%)	(46%)	(44%)
Democratic initiator	21 / 49	38 / 88	6 / 14	44 / 154	109 / 305
	(42%)	(43%)	(42%)	(28%)	(35%)
Total	54 / 117	115 / 230	22 / 45	156 / 427	347 / 819
	(46%)	(50%)	(48%)	(36%)	(42%)

putes involving democratic initiators and democratic targets have the lowest reciprocation rate, at 28 percent.

We also take into account a number of control variables that may influence a target state's decision to reciprocate a dispute. We measure these variables using the EUGene data management program (Bennett and Stam 2000). To control for relative military power, we create three dummy variables measuring whether states are major or minor powers. Major-major indicates that both states are major powers, major-minor indicates a major power initiator and minor power target, and minor-major indicates a minor power initiator and a major power target. We also include a control variable measuring the military balance between the initiator and target. This is a composite measure of system capability designed to capture which state has relatively greater fighting capabilities.[15] With this variable, increases indicate rises in the relative strength of the initiating state.

In addition, we include control variables measuring whether states in the conflict have a military alliance during the year of the dispute (ally), and whether states share land borders or are separated by twenty-five miles or less of water (contiguous), as well as dummy variables measuring the type of revision sought by the initiating state (territory revision, policy revision, regime-type revision, or other revision).[16] Following Jessica Weeks (2008), we include a control for similarity of alliance portfolios (how closely each state is aligned with the current leader of the international system) to indicate each state's evaluation of the status quo, consisting of two variables: status quo evaluation initiator and status quo evaluation target. To account for past relations between the two states, we include a further variable, peace days, which measures the time since their last conflict by using a decay function. Multiple studies have shown that the probability of dispute reciprocation decreases as time passes (Prins 2003; Raknerud and Hegre 1997). Last, because militarized interstate disputes vary markedly in intensity (Prins 2003; Toset, Gleditsch, and Hegre 2000), we include a control to capture salient differences across disputes. As Brandon Prins points out, militarized interstate disputes often merely represent cases in which fishing trawlers have been detained by national authorities, typically for violating maritime boundaries during fishing expeditions (2003, p. 76). We control for salience by including a dummy variable measuring whether the dispute involves a naval seizure.

In Table 3.2, we present tests of our argument holding constant the relevant control variables. Because our dependent variable is dichotomous, we use a logit model. In all of these tests, the excluded regime category is democratic initiator.

Models 1 and 2 confirm that the probability of reciprocation is higher when the initiating state is an authoritarian regime.[17] Controlling for the relevant variables, the probability that the target regime will reciprocate is greater when the initiating regime is authoritarian than when the initiating regime is democratic. This result is statistically significant and holds regardless of whether the sample is restricted to bilateral disputes. It is consistent with James Fearon's (1994) expectation that democratic regimes are better able to generate audience costs than are dictatorial regimes.

Models 3 and 4 explore how dictatorships vary with respect to the ability of their domestic audiences to effectively tie the hands of leaders. Regardless of whether multilateral disputes are excluded from the sample, personalist initiators yield the highest probability of reciprocation in comparison to democratic initiators, meaning that they have the lowest audience costs, as suggested previously. This result is statistically significant. Single-party initiators yield the next highest probability of reciprocation and the coefficient is also statistically significant, as expected. Though military initiators have a higher probability of reciprocation than democratic initiators, the result is not statistically significant, meaning that we cannot be sure that audience costs in military regimes are actually lower than in democracies.

Table 3.2 Initiator Regime Type and Probability of Dispute Reciprocation

Dependent Variable: Reciprocation	Model 1 (full sample)	Model 2 (bilateral MIDs)	Model 3 (full sample)	Model 4 (bilateral MIDS)
Constant	−1.83	−.47	−1.8***	−1.0**
	(.43)	(.40)	(.43)	(.48)
Regime type				
Authoritarian initiator	.68***	.48**	—	—
	(.22)	(.25)		
Personalist initiator	—	—	.88***	.58**
			(.26)	(.29)
Single-party initiator	—	—	.57**	.52*
			(.26)	(.30)
Military initiator	—	—	.50	.20
			(.34)	(.36)
Control variables				
Major-major	−.02	−.42	.08	−.44
	(.26)	(.30)	(.29)	(.34)
Major-minor	.06	−.07	.17	−.08
	(.26)	(.29)	(.28)	(.32)
Minor-major	.43	.30	.49*	.33
	(.30)	(.32)	(.30)	(.33)
Military balance	.72**	.49	.73**	.49
	(.36)	(.39)	(.36)	(.39)
Status quo evaluation initiator	.62*	.41	.57	.46
	(.35)	(.30)	(.37)	(.42)
Status quo evaluation target	−.67*	−.59	−.64*	−.63
	(.36)	(.42)	(.36)	(.43)
Territory revision	.39*	.09	.37	.11
	(.23)	(.24)	(.23)	(.25)
Policy revision	−1.32***	−1.4***	−1.3***	−1.4***
	(.20)	(.23)	(.20)	(23)
Regime-type revision	.30	.23	.29	.23
	(.46)	(.57)	(.45)	(.57)
Other revision	−.55	−1.1**	−.61	−1.2**
	(.49)	(.55)	(.49)	(.55)
Ally	.45*	.49*	.48*	.52*
	(.25)	(.29)	(.25)	(.29)
Contiguous	.48***	.37*	.51***	.37*
	(.18)	(.21)	(.18)	(.21)
Peace days	1.3***	.88***	1.3***	.90***
	(.26)	(.29)	(.26)	(.29)

(continues)

Table 3.2 continued

Dependent Variable: Reciprocation	Model 1 (full sample)	Model 2 (bilateral MIDs)	Model 3 (full sample)	Model 4 (bilateral MIDS)
Naval seizure	−1.14*** (.25)	−1.0*** (.26)	−1.1*** (.25)	−1.0*** (.27)
N	819	638	819	638
LL	−446.18	−360.39	−445.2	−359.84
χ^2	169.5	125.66	169.95	126.23
(p)	(.000)	(.000)	(.000)	(.000)
Pseudo R^2	.20	.17	.20	.17

Notes: Estimation is by logistic regression. Huber-White standard errors are in parentheses. "—" indicates not applicable. * $p < .10$, ** $p < .05$, *** $p < .01$.

(It is possible that that the small number of initiating military regimes in the sample increased the size of the standard error of this coefficient. It is also possible, however, that military initiators simply elicit rates of reciprocation comparable to those of democratic initiators because their threats are taken equally seriously.) Holding all other variables at their median (and ignoring statistical significance), the estimated probability of reciprocation is 72 percent for personalist initiators, 68 percent for single-party initiators, 63 percent for military initiators, and 55 percent for democratic initiators.[18]

The results as a whole confirm our prediction: when targeted, states are most likely to reciprocate when the initiating regime is a personalist dictatorship, followed by single-party dictatorship, and military dictatorship, and least likely to reciprocate against democratic regimes.[19] The difference between the reciprocation rates of democratic regimes and military regimes is not statistically significant. These results are consistent with our argument regarding differences in the ability of authoritarian audiences to impose high costs on leaders for poor foreign policy choices.

To ensure that our findings are robust to alternative measures of regime type, we also ran various tests controlling for measures of selectorate and winning coalition, as identified by Bruce Bueno de Mesquita and colleagues (2003), as well as a measure of the presence of a legislature, as emphasized by Jennifer Gandhi and Adam

Przeworski (2007). Our main results still hold.[20] Threats issued by personalist dictators appear to have the least credibility, followed by threats of single-party dictators, and lastly those of military dictators. As expected, military dictatorships are the most capable of signaling their resolve during interstate disputes, perhaps on a level comparable to that of democracies.

Unlike Weeks (2008), who finds that single-party dictatorships, military dictatorships, and democracies are about equally capable of generating audience costs,[21] our tests reveal that single-party dictatorships do not exhibit signaling abilities comparable to those of military dictatorships and democracies.[22] Single-party dictatorships have advantages in signaling when compared to personalist dictatorships, but have signaling disadvantages when compared to military dictatorships. This finding indicates that, in addition to elite coordination, elite control over the security apparatus is also critical for audience cost generation in dictatorships.

The tests presented here provide strong support for our argument about the way different forms of authoritarianism affect the capacity of support coalitions to discipline the dictator, and hence generate audience costs.

Conclusion

This chapter has analyzed how institutional differences across dictatorships affect the ability of dictators to signal that they mean what they say during international crises. We have highlighted the role of elite support coalitions in inflicting costs upon dictators for backing down on threats that they issue in public. The greater the ability of elites to overthrow the dictator, the greater their capacity to impose costs upon the leader for poor foreign policy choices. Because leaders of military regimes are more vulnerable to overthrow than are leaders of other kinds of autocracies, they face domestic costs that are not much different from those faced by democratic leaders, and hence their threats are credible. At the other end, personalist leaders face few credible threats of ouster. Consequently, domestic audience costs are low in personalist regimes, making their threats less credible. This argument leads to the expectation that threats from military regimes will elicit reciprocal hostile behavior less often than threats from single-party regimes, and that hostile responses will occur most often in response to threats from personalist regimes, since they face the lowest audience costs.

Empirical tests support this expectation. Some dictatorships are more capable than others of signaling their commitment during interstate disputes. Among dictatorships, threats issued by military dictatorships tend to be seen as the most credible, and threats issued by personalist dictatorships tend to be seen as the least credible. Crises are more likely to escalate when personalist dictatorships initiate them, followed by single-party dictatorships, and lastly military dictatorships.

These results help to explain Mark Peceny, Caroline Beer, and Shannon Sanchez-Terry's (2002) finding that there is a higher incidence of militarized interstate disputes among dyads that include a personalist dictatorship and a democracy. When personalist dictatorships instigate disputes, the probability of eliciting an escalatory response from the target is high. Because personalist dictatorships are more likely to initiate disputes with democracies than vice versa (Reiter and Stam 2003) *and* are more likely to elicit reciprocation, the probability that violent interstate conflict will occur between democracies and personalist dictatorships will be high.

Our findings lend further credence to the idea that the organizational foundations of authoritarian regimes are not all alike. The differences among them, as we have shown, influence the nature of leader-elite relations and, in turn, the ability of dictatorships to send credible signals of commitment during international crises.

Notes

1. Leaders may, however, choose to avoid making threats public in order to avoid facing these costs (Kurizaki 2007; Baum 2004a).

2. Alastair Smith (1998) shows, for example, that voters assume that leaders who back down after making a threat have low foreign policy competence.

3. Branislav Slantchev (2006) argues that democracies also vary in their ability to generate audience costs: those with more media protections better enable their citizens to sanction leaders.

4. However, the price of failure can be more severe for autocratic leaders, who potentially face much greater "audience costs" in the face of a coup (possibly fatal costs, such as execution) than do democratic leaders (Gowa 1995; Goemans 1995).

5. Qaddafi stated in 1987, for example: "The Arabs must possess the

atom bomb to defend themselves, until their numbers reach one thousand million and they learn to desalinate water and until they liberate Palestine" (Simons 1996, p. 257).

6. The ability to oust does not exhaust all potential costs that can be imposed on leaders domestically, such as protests, secession, and domestic turmoil. Our focus on the power to overthrow singles out the most important and salient of these costs.

7. Weeks also emphasizes two other factors in her argument: "whether the audience views backing down negatively" and "whether outsiders can observe the possibility of domestic sanctions for backing down" (2008, p. 35).

8. One might argue that other leaders view military dictators as likely to follow through with their threats not because of audience costs, but because military dictators have full control over the military. This argument, however, ignores the fact that personalist dictators also control the military, as well as a battery of paramilitary forces.

9. We do not examine the relationship between audience costs and conflict duration because it would be difficult to identify the true mechanism underlying the results of such tests. Peter Partell and Glenn Palmer (1999) and Joe Eyerman and Robert Hart (1996), for example, show that crises involving high–audience cost states are more likely to be short-lived and involve fewer rounds of escalation. The idea is that high–audience cost states generate costs at a quicker rate and therefore need fewer rounds to signal their intentions (Fearon 1994, p. 585). We exclude such a test here because the causal mechanism, though it could be the existence of political audience costs, could also be any of a variety of other factors (Schultz 2001, p. 34). We do not examine the relationship between audience costs and conflict initiation for the same reason. Though the theory implies that high–audience cost states will be less likely to initiate limited foreign policy probes (Fearon 1994, p. 591), it would be difficult to isolate in tests whether conflict initiation patterns are due to audience costs or other mechanisms, like executive constraints (Ireland and Gartner 2001) or sensitivity to public opinion (Baum 2004b).

10. The COW-MID dataset may not always be appropriate for addressing issues concerning conflict escalation (Gleditsch 1999). For example, during crises it may be difficult to identify which state is the initiator and which state is the target. As Brandon Prins points out, however: "At a snapshot in time, one state is faced with the decision to continue the militarized quarrel (certainly increasing the likelihood that it will end in war or some less severe, but still costly, form of armed violence) or capitulate and meet the demands of its adversary. Consequently, reciprocation can be viewed as an indication of state B's resolve, a costly step taken to influence the decision-making of state A" (2003, p. 73).

11. Brian Lai and Dan Slater (2006) also offer a typology of dictatorships for studying the conflict behavior of autocracies. We choose Geddes's because our focus is on the institutions that structure elite politics, rather than the extent to which dictatorships can enforce decisions via methods of social control, which is the basis for their classification.

12. The results are the same when states are coded as democratic with a score of 6 or higher.

13. The main results hold even in the larger sample that includes other forms of authoritarianism and transitional regimes.

14. Slantchev (2006) argues that the relationship between audience costs and regime type is nonlinear. By using dummy variables, rather than a linear scale of regime type, we do not constrain this relationship to be linear.

15. See Singer, Bremer, and Stuckley 1972 for a discussion of the indicators included in this measure.

16. We also tried including a variable measuring the distance between states, but the effect of the contiguity variable is stronger and more robust.

17. The variable, authoritarian initiator, includes personalist, military, and single-party regimes.

18. To estimate these values, we used CLARIFY (King, Tomz, and Wittenberg 2000).

19. To check whether unit-level characteristics of the target state systematically affect the likelihood that it will reciprocate, we also re-estimated Model 3 including dummy variables for each target state (Schultz 1999). Characteristics that systematically affect the probability that any single country will reciprocate should be captured by these dummy variables. Though the results weaken slightly, the magnitude and statistical significance of the regime initiator coefficients are virtually the same.

20. The results of these tests are available upon request.

21. Weeks also examines audience cost generation in new democracies and unstable nondemocracies and finds that leaders in these regimes face signaling difficulties comparable to those of leaders in personalist dictatorships.

22. Our tests primarily differ from those of Weeks in our inclusion of two additional appropriate control variables: whether the dispute involves a naval seizure, and the number of days that the dyad states have been at peace.

4

The Quality of
Military Intelligence

In 1989, US president George H. W. Bush publicly threatened Panamanian leader Manuel Noriega that the United States would invade Panama if Noriega did not acquiesce to US demands for democratic elections. Noriega dismissed Bush's words and US troops invaded soon afterward. Similarly, in 1994, US president Bill Clinton publicly warned Haitian leader Raoul Cédras that the United States would invade Haiti if Cédras and the Haitian military junta did not step down from power. Moments before US troops were set to attack, however, Cédras backed down and an agreement was reached. Why was conflict avoided in Haiti, but not in Panama? Why was Cédras able to assess that the threat from the United States was credible, but not Noriega?

Much emphasis in the conflict literature is placed on the ability of leaders to credibly signal their resolve during interstate disputes (e.g., Fearon 1994; Schultz 1998, 2001; Siegel 1997; Ramsay 2004; Smith 1998). Equally important, however, is the ability of states to accurately judge the credibility of threats sent to them by their adversaries. In order for signaling advantages to matter, target states must be able to correctly identify when signals are credible. As discussed in Chapter 3, leaders are better able to convey the credibility of their threats when they face high domestic costs for backing down on them (Fearon 1994). Yet not all states seem equally capable of gauging the credibility of threats, as the differing outcomes in Panama and Haiti make clear.

In this chapter, we examine how institutional differences across dictatorships influence the quality of their military intelligence channels. We argue that the lower the quality of the military intelligence received, the less likely leaders are to accurately read signals sent to them. High-quality intelligence is essential for successful foreign policy ventures. Without accurate information about enemy states, it is difficult for leaders to correctly gauge enemy intentions. Poor-quality intelligence also makes it harder for leaders to accurately assess their own strategic and defense capabilities. It increases the likelihood that leaders will misread signals and make foreign policy errors.

In dictatorships, leaders obtain sensitive information from the same group that can oust them: their elite advisory group. Paradoxically, the caliber of intelligence is likely to be poorer when leaders control membership to this group. This is true for two reasons: (1) dictators, when given the choice, will choose to surround themselves with low-skilled individuals, people who are less likely to overthrow them, but also less competent; and (2) elites, when it is easy for the dictator to casually dismiss them, will be less likely to relay unpleasant information to the dictator, out of fear of reprisal.[1] Dictators who have greater control over the selection of their advisory group are more likely to end up surrounded by "yes men," individuals who say whatever the dictator wants to hear in order to stay in his good favor.

As discussed in Chapter 2, personalist dictators have greater control over the selection of their advisers than do military or single-party dictators. In personalist dictatorships, leaders are not constrained by a military or party apparatus when it comes to choosing who will compose their elite support coalition, and they have more direct control over promotions. Personalist elites do not share membership in an institutionalized party or military, which decreases their bargaining power relative to that of the dictator. By contrast, single-party and military dictators must adhere to party or military guidelines for promotions when selecting elites and have less direct control over who they can appoint and dismiss. Single-party and military elites share membership in the party and military, respectively, which "unionizes" them and increases their bargaining power relative to that of the dictator. Because personalist dictators have greater control over the composition of their elite advisory group than do single-party or military dictators, they should receive poorer-quality intelligence from their advisers and, as a result, be more likely to err in their reading of signals during interstate disputes.[2]

Based on a case study of Iraq under Saddam Hussein and quantitative tests of our expectation, we find that personalist dictatorships interpret dispute signals with greater error than do other forms of dictatorship. Though, on average, regimes are equally likely to accurately read the signals sent to them, the behavior of personalist dictatorships from one dispute to the next is more erratic than that of other authoritarian regimes. The implications of this finding are clear: when leaders embroil themselves in conflicts with personalist dictators, they should not assume that they are dealing with well-informed and predictable foes.

How Authoritarianism Influences the Accuracy of Intelligence

In dictatorships, leaders obtain information and advice from the same group that can oust them: the elite coalition. This group serves as the dictator's main information channel for domestic and international security concerns. The institutional structure of the dictatorship matters because it affects the ability of leaders to control who will compose their elite advisory group. Paradoxically, when leaders have power over the selection of their elite advisory group, it decreases the caliber of the military intelligence they receive. Control over selection has two consequences, both of which lessen the quality of intelligence: (1) leaders will select less qualified individuals because they are unlikely to have the skills or desire to oust them, and (2) elites will be less likely to report to the dictator information that he does not want to hear, out of fear of reprisal.

As argued in Chapter 2, personalist dictators have greater control over the selection of their advisers than do military or single-party dictators. This should make them less likely to receive accurate information during interstate disputes and more likely to commit foreign policy blunders.

Incentives for Selecting Low-Skilled Elites

With full rein over the composition of their support group, personalist dictators can select low-skilled individuals who are unlikely to oust them. In fact, dictators—when they have a choice—often choose individuals based on their loyalty rather than their competence (Egorov and Sonin 2006).[3] Advisers who are competent are typically removed from the dictator's advisory group because they serve as potential threats to the dictator's power.

Examples of this abound. In Uganda, most of the high-ranking officials under Idi Amin were illiterate, mainly because he was resentful of those who were better educated (Ravenhill 1974, p. 248). He even accused his top brigadier, Moses Ali, his army chief of staff, Isaac Lumago, and his police commissioner, Kassimu Obura, of being "too competent" (Basajabka et al. 1994, p. 122). Amin selected advisers without any consideration of their qualifications: "Fickle appointments characterize all of his relationships such as the brief career of Toro Princess Elizabeth Bagaya who was a former fashion model who became Amin's Foreign Minister. She debuted at the UN General Assembly in a tightly fitted gold gown. Her downfall was due to Amin's accusation that she had made love to an unknown European in a toilet. She escaped after being detained under house arrest in 1975" (Legum 1997, p. 257). Similarly, in the Dominican Republic under Rafael Trujillo, loyalty was the key requirement for even the highest political posts. Jacinto Bienvenido Peynado was appointed vice president "due to his loyalty and the fact that he preferred leisure to power" (Crassweller 1966, p. 167). The same was true of General José Estrella, whose loyalty was "of a kind not often encountered except among four-legged animals. His mentality was rude and rustic, totally unsophisticated" (Crassweller 1966, p. 185). Pol Pot of Cambodia also valued loyalty over knowledge. Everyone who had a higher education or public service experience was executed upon Pol Pot's assumption to power (Kiernan 2004).

When they have a choice, leaders typically prefer loyal—as opposed to competent—elite advisers, because they view members of their advisory group as potential rivals. Such was the case with Jean-Bédel Bokassa of the Central African Republic: "Despite his secondary education and a certain cosmopolitan veneer, he also felt threatened, at least to some extent, by more qualified personnel, even as he craved their adulation and constant glorification" (Decalo 1985, p. 222). In Libya, Muammar Qaddafi developed a unique system for deterring potential rivals. He ensured that members of his elite chain of command were assigned a misleading set of ranks and titles. As Craig Black writes, "No one outside Libya—and perhaps even inside—knows for sure who controls exactly what. The vagueness and obscurity of this system is said to be of [Qaddafi's] own design, intended to confuse potential competitors within the regime" (2000,

p. 10). While such tactics may protect the dictator's hold on power, they also lower the skill level of the dictator's elite advisory group.[4]

Disincentives for Relaying Accurate Intelligence

Because personalist dictators can select (and purge) members of their elite advisory group as they please (as discussed in Chapter 2), elites tend to be less likely to report to the dictator unpleasant information, out of fear that they will be punished for doing so.[5] In the Philippines under Ferdinand Marcos, for example, cabinet members could not bring themselves to speak out against his excesses (Hawes 1995, p. 157). Those he appointed reported that "loyalty dictated that they would not state anything to contradict Marcos or say anything to protest his interference" (Hawes 1995, p. 158). Elite fear of reprisal is often justified. Uganda's Amin would personally beat ministers who were doubtful of his "facts" (Decalo 1985, p. 227). When the minister of finance reported that cotton production had declined by 60 percent, he was never heard from again ("Fall of Idi Amin" 1979). Bokassa used amputations as a form of punishment. Being part of his support group was a risky job; individuals risked death and torture if they displeased him (Titley 1997, p. 45). When leaders control the fates of elites, elites are less likely to relay information that their leaders do not want to hear.[6]

The Consequences of Control

When dictators have greater control over the selection of elites to their advisory group, as in personalist dictatorships, elites are more likely to be incompetent and less likely to report to the dictator unfavorable information, decreasing the quality of intelligence that the dictator receives.[7] In Zaire, for example, Mobutu Sese Seko set in place calculated measures to limit the professional competence of his advisers. As a result, during multiple conflicts with other states, he was never privy to accurate intelligence regarding either his own military capabilities or the military capabilities of his adversaries (Afoaku 1999). Isolated from reality and surrounded by flatterers, personalist dictators "frequently engage in self-delusional fantasies—that the intervention will not really occur, that some third force will halt the standoff before it runs to its logical conclusion, or that their own military forces will somehow deter the enemy" (Carothers 2003, p. 59).

These problems are compounded when leaders themselves are unskilled in foreign policy matters. As Michael Handel wrote, "an adviser's role is even more crucial when the leader he serves has no prior experience with intelligence work" (1989, p. 15). Uganda's Amin, for example, was incapable of grasping complex matters and, because of this, dissolved his advisory bodies to avoid his own discomfort during formal meetings (Decalo 1985, p. 227). Instead, he turned to his cronies, drinking companions, and a group of trustworthy commanders for advice. After discussing policies for hours with these individuals, the policies that resulted were "later forgotten, unrecorded, irrelevant and not implementable" (Decalo 1985, p. 227). Ultimately, Amin relied on his own gut reactions to make decisions. As Christopher Andrew and Julie Elkner (2003) point out, in personalist dictatorships, leaders often are personally involved with the work of intelligence agencies, which can lead to serious errors in the identification of targets and threats and in the processing of information.

In military and single-party dictatorships, by contrast, elites are bound together by the institution that unites them, the military and the party respectively. Just as employers facing a unionized labor market have less autonomy in hiring, leaders in military and single-party regimes have less control over membership of their elite advisory group. Leaders generally cannot select individuals based on the likelihood of loyalty, but rather must bargain with elites over membership in the ruling body. Military and single-party dictators also have less control over who they can dismiss, just as employers facing a unionized work force have less control over dismissals. They are less capable of removing elites from the coalition solely because those elites have reported to them undesirable information.

Elite selection in military and single-party dictatorships is more likely to be determined by military and party guidelines for promotions than by the leader's preferences. In military dictatorships, elites operate in a domestic environment that is controlled by the military apparatus; in single-party dictatorships, elites operate in a domestic environment dominated by the party. Elites are often forced to work their way up the military or party ladder to attain their positions. By the time they reach "elite" status, individuals have typically spent many years working within the military or party organization. Leaders may try to influence promotions in the military or within the party, but they do not usually have absolute power over promotions, as military or party guidelines carry greater weight. As a result, elites are more likely to be high-skilled and competent, because they typically have been vetted by the military or party apparatus.

Lack of accurate intelligence—or the decision to ignore it—should increase the likelihood that personalist dictators will commit foreign policy errors. High-quality intelligence apparatus are crucial for correctly assessing enemy intentions and capabilities, as well as one's own capabilities. In personalist dictatorships, leaders do not bargain with a "unionized" elite support group like dictators do in single-party or military regimes. As a result, personalist dictators have greater bargaining power relative to their supporters, and greater control over who they can appoint and dismiss. This has two interrelated consequences for the caliber of intelligence they receive. First, personalist dictators will appoint individuals based on loyalty over competence. Second, elites will refrain from reporting accurate information to the dictator out of fear of being dismissed. Both of these factors decrease the quality of intelligence that personalist dictators receive and, consequently, increase the likelihood that personalist dictators will misread signals sent to them during interstate disputes.

Saddam's Iraq: Errors in Judgment

The case of Iraq under Saddam Hussein illustrates these factors well. Hussein lived in fear of attempted coups. Recent Iraqi history had proven that coups were often the norm. Saddam trusted no one and relied solely on his family or members of his tribe. The most important posts in Iraq—that he did not himself occupy—were given to Hussein's relatives. The Revolutionary Guard, for example, was controlled by Hussein's son Qusay (al-Marashi 2002); the Fedayeen was controlled by his eldest son, Uday (Woods et al. 2006, p. 53). Neither son had the experience or qualifications necessary to oversee elite military forces. The commander of the Special Republic Guard, the most elite force that Hussein had at his disposal, was Barzan Abd al-Ghafur, Hussein's cousin and a man considered lacking in aptitude (Woods et al. 2006, p. 57).

With Hussein, loyalty trumped competence. As Ali Hassan al-Majid, better known as Chemical Ali, stated: "Saddam was always wary of intelligent people. While Saddam liked having men around him with strong personalities, he did not like for those men to show off" (Woods et al. 2006, p. 56). In the end, the advisers who surrounded

Hussein were sycophantic and terrified of contradicting him or being perceived as threats to his power. In Hussein's Iraq, "real knowledge was not a prized commodity" (Woods et al. 2006, pp. 11–12).

In addition to surrounding himself with poorly trained advisers, Hussein preferred to make many decisions on his own with little consultation or deliberation (al-Marashi 2002). Occasionally he would consult small groups of family members or longtime associates, but this was atypical. The decision to invade Kuwait, for example, was made after discussions with only one individual: his son-in-law. The decision to invade Iran—a war that cost the lives of hundreds of thousands of Iraqis—was made while traveling to a resort (Post and Baram 2002). Hussein preferred to reach decisions on his own even though he had little experience in foreign affairs, having barely traveled outside of the Arab world (Post 1991, p. 6). This decisionmaking style and lack of experience, coupled with Hussein's poor choice of advisers, resulted in the enactment of policies that were poorly formulated and, ultimately, costly. As Jerrold Post wrote, "the combination of a limited international perspective and a sycophantic leadership circle . . . led him to miscalculate" (1991, p. 6).

Hussein's advisers had few incentives to report truthful information to him, as the penalties for doing so, should that information be deemed unpleasant, were harsh. The mere suggestion that US tanks were superior to Iraqi tanks, for example, resulted in a year in prison for one of Hussein's advisers (Fleishman 2004, p. 1). Tariz Aziz, the foreign minister under Hussein, commented that if military leaders disappeared, "one did not ask to know what happened, since it was known that the security services had dealt with the unfortunate individual" (Woods et al. 2006, p. 7). Individuals who offered ideas of their own to Hussein were often dismissed. This ensured that Hussein never had to deal with information that he did not want to hear (Handel 1989, p. 23). When the Iran-Iraq War started going poorly for Iraq, for example, Hussein decided that he wanted to put an end to the conflict. At a cabinet meeting, he asked his ministers for advice as to how he should go about doing so. His minister of health suggested Hussein step down from power temporarily, in compliance with Iran's stated terms for peace, with the idea being that Hussein would immediately return to power once the war ended. Hussein thanked the minister for his honesty, arrested him, chopped up his body into pieces, and returned it to his wife in a duffle bag (see Woods et al. 2006, p. 7; Post 1991, p. 6). Hussein's other ministers learned quickly that honesty had high costs.

Lies became much safer than truths in Iraq. As William Branigan wrote, "One lied to the other from the first lieutenant up, until it reached Saddam" (2003, p. A25). A Military Industrial Commission annual report of investments made in 2002, for example, showed that Iraq had more than 170 research projects with an estimated budget of about 1.5 percent of Iraq's gross domestic product (GDP) (Woods, Lacey, and Murray 2006). Yet most of these projects were shams. Iraqi officials were too afraid to initiate weapons programs that they knew the country did not have the capacity to develop. Hussein was updated regularly with fake plans and designs as officials sought to demonstrate the ostensible progress being made. As Kevin Woods, James Lacey, and Williamson Murray state, "This constant stream of false reporting accounts for why many of Saddam's calculations on operational, strategic, and political issues made perfect sense to him" (2006, p. 8).

In order to please Hussein, elites often overestimated Iraqi capabilities and understated those of the enemy. Hussein was led to believe that his Al-Quds army was 7 million members strong. In reality, there were only 500,000 members (Woods et al. 2006, pp. 48–49). In order to stay in Hussein's good graces, military units reported that their training was impeccable and scientists claimed that they had their hands on the latest and greatest weapons technology (Gerstein 2003). Any military plan suggested by Hussein was greeted with unanimous enthusiasm from his advisers and military generals, no matter how ridiculous it seemed. During the 1990 Gulf War, for example, once combat operations began, Iraqi commanders stuck solely to giving Hussein good news and praising his successes. On the third day of the air campaign, Hussein's minister of information, Latif Jassim, declared (to a confused international press) that Iraq had been victorious. Jassim claimed that coalition forces had expected Iraq to fall and that each day Iraq defied the West was evidence of the magnitude of his country's strength (Post 1991, p. 12). Similarly, during the 2003 Iraq War, Hussein's minister of information, Mohammad Saeed al-Sahaf, reported to the international press endless Iraqi successes against coalition forces. On March 31, he stated: "Our people from all sectors, fighters, courageous tribesmen, as well as the fighters of the valiant Arab Socialist Ba'ath Party fought battles and pushed the enemy back into the desert. . . . Now hundreds of thousands of the fighters of the valiant Iraqi people are distributed in all places. . . . We destroyed 13 tanks, 8 tracked personnel carriers and 6 half-tracked vehicles" ("Iraq's al-Sahhaf Holds News Conference on

Military Situation" 2003). In the West, these comments were viewed as "palpable nonsense" (Woods, Lacey, and Murray 2006, p. xix). Around the same time, the Iraqi foreign minister was directed to tell the French and Russian governments that Iraq would accept only an "unconditional withdrawal" of US forces, because "Iraq is now winning . . . and the United States has sunk in the mud of defeat" (Woods, Lacey, and Murray 2006, p. 4). Perhaps surprisingly, evidence indicates that Hussein believed every word of this propaganda (Woods et al. 2006, p. 32). Meanwhile, US tanks were a hundred miles south of Baghdad, refueling and rearming for their final push (Woods et al. 2006, p. 31).

Hussein's obsession with survival in office resulted in the creation of an intelligence apparatus with disincentives for reporting truths. After he invaded Kuwait on August 2, 1990, for example, he was certain that no retaliatory measures would be taken. He maintained this confidence even after US president George H. W. Bush announced on television on September 11 that US forces were ready to invade. On January 12, 1991, Congress passed a resolution authorizing Bush to do so (US Department of Defense 2000). Still, according to Hussein's calculations, Bush was bluffing. He believed that the United States posed no serious threat to Iraq. Once the US-led coalition attacked, Hussein was left in shock by the magnitude of the destruction caused by US air strikes (Perry 1991, p. 1; Post 1991, p. 11). When the Gulf War ended in February 1991, an estimated 200,000 Iraqis had been killed (US Department of Defense 2000).

The Iraq War provides yet another example of miscalculations on the part of Hussein. This case proved to be even more costly for Saddam, however, leading to his eventual ouster and execution. A few weeks before the US invasion in 2003, Hussein refused to believe that the United States would use ground forces in Iraq. Iraqi intelligence reports indicated that the real danger was Iran, not the United States, even though US president George W. Bush publicly stated on television on March 6, 2003, that war with Iraq was imminent (Woods et al. 2006).[8] Hussein believed that if US troops did invade, they either would be severely defeated or would leave due to international pressure (Beeston 2004). He was convinced that his forces were far superior to those of the US-led coalition and that there would be a "heroic resistance" that would "inflict such enormous losses on the Americans that they would stop their advance" (Woods et al. 2006, p. 27). Even when it became obvious that the

United States was going to attack Iraq, Hussein wholeheartedly believed that he was not personally at risk (see Woods et al. 2006). According to Ibrahim Ahmad Abd al-Satter, chief of staff of Iraq's armed forces, Hussein was assured that the United States would not succeed in removing him from power. As Matthew Schofield (2006) noted, "No Iraqi leaders had believed coalition forces would ever reach Baghdad" (Woods and Pease 2006, p. 31).[9]

As the war progressed and things took a turn for the worse in Iraq, Iraqi officials continued to report Iraqi successes. In a memorandum dated April 6, 2003, Iraq's Ministry of Defense informed subordinate units that "we are doing great," while reminding all staff officers to "avoid exaggerating the enemy's capabilities" (Woods, Lacey, and Murray 2006, p. 25). That same day, Hussein gave orders to deploy formations that no longer existed! On April 7, 2003, al-Sahaf, the Iraqi minister of information, stated that US forces were besieged in Baghdad City: "Most of them were dealt with. We made them drink poison last night and the great forces of leader Saddam Hussein have taught them a lesson that history will never forget" ("Iraqi Information Minister Denies Presence of US Forces in Baghdad" 2003). Meanwhile, Iraq's military forces were near collapse, with coalition forces having destroyed nearly all division headquarters. But any information that might contradict the military genius of Hussein could not be revealed (Eisenstadt and Pollack 2001).

Hussein's errors in judgment during the conflicts with the United States were not his first. Several commentators have noted that Hussein's decision to invade Iran in 1980 was due to errors in intelligence and poor judgment. As Jack Levy and Mike Froelick wrote, "the war would not have occurred without Iraq's fatal misperceptions and miscalculations. Iraq underestimated Iran's military capabilities relative to its own, the unifying effect of the war on Iranian society, the military consequences of revolutionary fervor and the resolve of the Khomeini regime" (1985, p. 134). Though Iran was in the midst of its revolution, Hussein underrated Iran's capacity for resistance, an enormous miscalculation that was extremely costly (Pollack 2002, pp. 258–259). As Phebe Marr put it, the war with Iran was "the result of poor political judgment and miscalculation on the part of Saddam Hussein" (1985, p. 234).

In personalist dictatorships, elites do not bargain with the dictator as a collective. This drives down the price of their support and gives the dictator a greater say in their selection. As the case of Iraq under

Saddam Hussein illustrates, rather than being forced to abide by party or military guidelines for promotion, personalist dictators can choose whomever they please to be part of their advisory group. They often select those individuals who are least likely to oust them, with loyalty being a more valued trait than competence. Because personalist dictators can also dismiss their subordinates at will, elites are less likely to report to them information their leaders do not want to hear. Both of these factors decrease the quality of intelligence that personalist dictators receive and increase the likelihood that personalist dictators will commit foreign policy errors.

Testing the Argument

We argue that personalist dictators are more likely than single-party or military dictators to receive low-quality intelligence and, as a result, make foreign policy mistakes. Because it is impossible to know with certainty the logic behind leaders' choices during inter-state disputes, we instead test an implication of our argument. If personalist dictators have more difficulty gauging the credibility of threats sent to them than do military or single-party dictators, then they should exhibit greater uncertainty in their responses to threats. Therefore, building on the quantitative models used in Chapter 3, we test whether personalist dictatorships display more uncertainty in their reactions to enemy provocations.[10]

We examine how regimes respond to threats (whether they choose to reciprocate or not), given the audience cost level of the initiating state. If there is no difference in the quality of intelligence that different types of dictators receive, then there should be no difference in their responses to threats. When a high–audience cost state issues a threat, all states should back down in the dispute.[11] When a low–audience cost state issues a threat, all states should move to escalate the dispute. If our argument is true, however, personalist dictatorships should exhibit more uncertainty in their responses to threats than do military or single-party dictatorships, occasionally backing down in disputes when the threat is a bluff and occasionally escalating disputes when the threat is genuine.

To test our expectation, we look at levels of uncertainty in the responses of target states to threats sent to them during interstate disputes. Following research that associates increasing uncertainty with greater error variance (Alvarez and Brehm 1995; Downs and Rocke 1979; Reed 2003a, 2003b), we posit that low-quality intelligence increases the noise in the target's choice of the optimal response. We look at the variance of the error in the probability that target states will reciprocate the threats of challengers. This is essentially a test of whether there are differences in the heterogeneity of responses to signals of resolve across types of targeted regimes.

Because of this, we use a heteroskedastic probit model.[12] This is a test of the variance of the probability of reciprocation across regimes rather than a test of the mean. This model is basically a heteroskedastic regression for dichotomous dependent variables. The heteroskedastic probit model simultaneously estimates both the mean and the variance of the error term as a function of a set of predictors using maximum-likelihood estimation.[13] We expect that personalist dictatorships should exhibit greater error variance in response to threats sent to them than do military or single-party dictatorships.

In our tests, the dependent variable is the same as in Chapter 3: the probability of reciprocation. In Model 1, we estimate the mean using the same control variables as in Chapter 3. In Model 2, we include, in addition, dummy variables measuring the regime type of the target, also described in Chapter 3. For both models, we estimate the variance of the error term using the target-regime dummy variables. Positive coefficients for these variables indicate a positive relationship between the regime type of the target state and the magnitude of the variance of the error term. In the mean equation, democratic initiator is the excluded category, and in the variance equation, democratic target is the excluded category.[14] We present the results of these tests in Table 4.1.

The results of these tests provide positive support for our argument. With respect to the variance of the error term, in Model 1 the coefficient for personalist target is the largest and is statistically significant. Personalist targets exhibit the greatest variance in the probability that they will reciprocate disputes, indicating that personalist dictators are more uncertain in their estimation of the credibility of signals than are leaders of other regime types.[15] The coefficient of single-party target is also positive, though not statistically significant. The coefficient of military target is the smallest, negative, and not statistically different from 0.

The results in Model 2 are virtually the same.[16] Model 2 also reveals, however, that dictatorships on average do not exhibit differences in their responses. When estimating the mean—or the probabil-

Table 4.1 Variance in Probability of Dispute Reciprocation

	Model 1 (heteroskedastic probit)	Model 2 (heteroskedastic probit)	Model 3 (probit)
Dependent variable: reciprocation			
Constant	−1.2***	−1.33***	−1.12***
	(.30)	(.29)	(.26)
Regime variables			
Personalist initiator	.63***	.60***	.52***
	(.18)	(.18)	(.15)
Single-party initiator	.34**	.31*	.33**
	(.18)	(.18)	(.15)
Military initiator	.33	.35	.30
	(.24)	(.22)	(.20)
Personalist target	—	−.13	
		(.33)	—
Single-party target	—	.17	
		(.16)	—
Military target	—	.13	
		(.17)	—
Control variables			
Major-major	.09	.06	.05
	(.20)	(.20)	(.18)
Major-minor	.16	.16	.10
	(.19)	(.19)	(.16)
Minor-major	.40*	.36	.32*
	(.22)	(.23)	(.17)
Military balance	.37	.38	.44**
	(.25)	(.25)	(.22)
Status quo evaluation initiator	.27	.17	.33
	(.25)	(.28)	(.22)
Status quo evaluation target	−.36	−.24	−.38*
	(.25)	(.28)	(.22)
Territory revision	.27*	.27*	.22*
	(.16)	(.16)	(.13)
Policy revision	−.93***	−.92***	−.81***
	(.15)	(.15)	(.12)
Regime-type revision	.29	.23	.18
	(.33)	(.31)	(.27)
Other revision	−.30	−.27	−.36
	(.31)	(.31)	(.29)
Ally	.40**	.41**	.29**
	(.18)	(.18)	(.15)

(continues)

Table 4.1   continued

	Model 1 (heteroskedastic probit)	Model 2 (heteroskedastic probit)	Model 3 (probit)
Contiguous	.43***	.40***	.30***
	(.12)	(.13)	(.10)
Peace days	.93***	.96***	.78***
	(.19)	(.19)	(.15)
Naval seizure	−.74***	−.73***	−.66***
	(.19)	(.17)	(.14)
Dependent variable: variance of error term of reciprocation			
Personalist target	.92***	.93**	—
	(.38)	(.39)	
Single-party target	.26	.22	—
	(.20)	(.20)	
Military target	−.35	−.40	—
	(.33)	(.32)	
N	819	819	819
LL	−438.12	−437.21	−444.74
χ^2	135.12	129.21	191.69
(p)	(.000)	(.000)	(.000)

Notes: "—" indicates not applicable. * $p < .10$, ** $p < .05$, *** $p < .01$.

ity of reciprocation—none of the coefficients of the target dummy variables are statistically significant. On average, all regimes have similar probabilities of reciprocating disputes when targeted, though there is greater variation in the probability of reciprocation among personalist dictatorships than among other regime types.[17]

Last, nonconstant variances in the error term of a probit model may lead to incorrect standard errors as well as biased and inconsistent estimates of the parameters (Yatchew and Griliches 1985). Therefore it is important to ensure that the estimates obtained from the models in Chapter 3 do not differ markedly from the estimates obtained using the heteroskedastic probit model. Since probit coefficients are different from those obtained from logit, in Model 3 we re-estimate the key model used in Chapter 3, using probit to serve as a baseline.

The coefficients of the regime-initiator variables estimated with the basic probit model (Model 3) are similar to those estimated with the heteroskedastic probit model (Model 1), with the exception that in the latter model the difference between the coefficients of personalist initiator and single-party initiator is slightly larger and the difference between the coefficients of single-party initiator and military initiator is slightly smaller. Any nonconstant variance in the reciprocation rates of target states does not appear to be biasing the estimates of the coefficients of the regime-initiator variables in the basic probit model.[18]

Heteroskedastic probit models can also be sensitive to misspecification (Achen 2002). We follow Randall Blimes (2006) and test the robustness of the heteroskedastic probit results by using a probit model and splitting the sample according to the regime type of the target state. Because we are interested in how personalist targets differ in their responses to threats compared to military and single-party targets, we break the sample into two smaller subsamples consisting of solely militarized interstate disputes in which the target state is a personalist dictatorship, and solely militarized interstate disputes in which the target state is a military or single-party dictatorship.[19] We run probit models for each subsample using the variables in Model 1. We expect that in the personalist subsample, the standard errors around the coefficients for the explanatory variables will be larger

Table 4.2   Changes in Probit Standard Errors by Regime Type of Target State

| | Standard Error | | | |
	Personalist	Military/ Single- Party	Difference	Percentage Decrease
Personalist initiator	.36	.28	−.08	29
Single-party initiator	.40	.24	−.16	67
Military initiator	.50	.38	−.12	32
Military balance	.44	.34	−.10	29
Status quo evaluation initiator	.68	.44	−.24	55
Status quo evaluation target	.75	.48	−.27	56
Territory revision	.30	.21	−.09	43
Policy revision	.23	.18	−.05	28
Regime-type revision	.54	.28	−.26	93
Other revision	.63	.49	−.14	29
Ally	.25	.25	0	0
Contiguous	.30	.17	−.13	76
Peace days	.34	.23	−.11	48
Naval seizure	.39	.22	−.17	77

than those in the military/single-party subsample.[20] We present these results in Table 4.2.

In every case but one, the personalist subsample generates larger standard errors than the military/single-party subsample. The average decrease in the standard error of coefficients from the personalist subsample to the military/single-party subsample is 45 percent.

The tests presented here indicate that the behavior of personalist dictatorships, when targeted, is more unpredictable than the behavior of other regimes. Personalist dictatorships exhibit a greater uncertainty or "error" in their interpretation of signals sent to them than do other kinds of regimes. With poor intelligence, as in personalist regimes, signals may get through, but they also may not.[21] Low-quality intelligence increases a target's uncertainty regarding the credibility of the initiator state's signal. As a result, personalist dictatorships exhibit greater error variance in the probability that they will reciprocate disputes in comparison to other regimes.

Conclusion

In this chapter we have argued that the institutional structure of dictatorships influences the quality of the military intelligence that dictators receive from their elite advisers. We have posited that greater control over the selection of advisers decreases the quality of the information relayed to leaders. Because personalist leaders have near total control over the composition of their advisory group, they typically select low-skilled individuals who pose little challenge to them. Idi Amin, Jean-Bédel Bokassa, and Teodoro Obiang Nguema, for example, were all known to shun expert opinion: "their immediate reference groups, their trusted lieutenants, were the sycophants, the self-seeking aides who were often unlettered" (Decalo 1985, p. 226). Such individuals are less likely to report unpleasant information to the dictator, for fear of the leader's reaction. As a result, the quality of intelligence should be poorer in personalist dictatorships than in other forms of dictatorship. With poor intelligence, personalist dictators should be more likely to misread signals sent to them during interstate disputes and commit foreign policy mistakes.

Based on our quantitative tests examining levels of uncertainty in regimes' responses to signals sent to them during interstate conflicts, we find that in comparison to single-party, military, and democratic regimes, personalist dictatorships are significantly less predictable when targeted; they exhibit more "error" in their responses to signals than do other regimes. Though the aggregate outcome is not differentiable from that of other regimes, there is greater variance in the behavior of personalist targets. Personalist dictatorships exhibit more heterogeneity than do other regime types in the probability that they will escalate disputes when targeted. We argue that this is because low-quality intelligence increases the noise in the target's choice of the optimal response. Personalist dictators are less predictable in their "reading" of signals because they do not consistently receive high-quality intelligence from their subordinates.

These results lend support to recent studies stressing the importance of considering differences in the variance in international conflict behavior. As William Reed points out, "One weakness of previous empirical studies of conflict onset is their assumption that there is no observed heterogeneity in the conflict data" (2003a, p. 55); the current literature considers "variation in conflict behavior only in the mean rather than in the variance" (2003b, p. 638). This is true even though evidence is building that heterogeneous data are the norm in international politics (Box-Steffensmeier and Zorn 2002; Lemke 2002; Reed 2003a, 2003b). Many political science phenomena produce changes in the variance, not in the mean, suggesting that there is much to be learned by modeling variance.[22] As Bear Braumoeller notes, "thinking in terms of variance-altering causation opens up a new theoretical dimension, one that has been largely neglected" (2006, p. 273).[23]

Our findings suggest that signals of credibility are only effective to the extent that targets are able to read them. Given that there are systematic differences in the responses of target states to signals like audience costs, failing to account for them may lead to incorrect estimates of the ability of initiator states to issue signals of commitment.

The tests presented here help to explain why we occasionally see personalist dictators blatantly disregarding the public warnings of democrats, as Manuel Noriega did with Bush Sr. and Saddam Hussein did with Bush Sr. and Bush Jr. Due to greater uncertainty surrounding their estimates of a challenger's resolve, personalist dictators may escalate disputes in which challengers have signaled that their threat is credible, and personalist dictators may back down in disputes in which challengers are bluffing. Our findings suggest that responses to aggressive acts carried out by autocratic governments should depend on the kind of dictatorship that perpetrates them. In disputes with personalist dictators, leaders should by no means assume that they are dealing with predictable, well-informed adversaries who will follow the traditional rules of the international relations game.

Notes

1. "Unpleasant information" refers to any information that is contrary to what the dictator wants to hear. Whether this information is considered by observers to be "good news" or "bad news" is inconsequential; what matters is whether it displeases the dictator.

2. As with all leaders, personalist dictators, even if they do receive accurate information from their advisers, may choose to ignore it.

3. As Georgy Egorov and Konstantin Sonin point out, "while incompetent ministers are not completely unusual in democratic countries, most historians and political scientists would agree that dictatorships are especially marred by incompetence" (2006, p. 2).

4. As Herbert Howe emphasizes, competence and political loyalty are often mutually exclusive (2001, p. 11).

5. Even in democratic regimes, where the costs of upsetting the leader are lower, "subordinates . . . tend to bias messages so as to minimize distress to their superiors" (Betts 1981, p. 555).

6. One could argue that leaders would want to hear "bad news" because if they ignore it they risk losing office. This is not necessarily contrary to our argument. As mentioned previously, elites will relay to the dictator whatever it is that he wants to hear, whether good or bad.

7. Use of the strategy of divide and conquer—popular among personalist dictators, as discussed in Chapter 2—can also harm intelligence capabilities, by leading to "the unnecessary duplication of efforts and the inability to get a more complete picture of the enemy" (Handel 1989, p. 23).

8. Bush also stated clearly on multiple other occasions the conditions under which a US invasion would occur.

9. Hussein's belief that he would survive the war helps to explain why he did not torch Iraqi oil fields or open the dams, as many experts had predicted.

10. Poor intelligence in personalist dictatorships does not necessarily mean that personalist dictators will be overly optimistic about the likelihood of their successes during crises. Poor intelligence is not the same thing as "good news." Elites will relay to personalist dictators whatever it is that they want to hear, regardless of whether it is good or bad. In personalist dictatorships, elites will support the dictator's position whatever it may be, leading to a weaker filtering of intelligence and greater uncertainty during crises.

11. As discussed in Chapter 3, according to the audience cost theory (Fearon 1994), high–audience cost states are better able to signal their commitment during interstate disputes than are low–audience cost states. This implies that high–audience cost states will elicit lower rates of reciprocation from their targets (Schultz 1999).

12. This method, based on Andrew Harvey (1976) and developed by William Greene (2000, pp. 649–651), was first implemented in the political science literature by R. Michael Alvarez and John Brehm (1995).

13. In the basic probit model, the unobserved errors (or the latent errors) are assumed to be distributed N (θ, σ^2). In the heteroskedastic probit model, however, the unobserved errors are assumed to be distributed N (θ, $\exp(z_i\gamma)^2$), where z_i is a vector of covariates of the ith observation that define groups with different error variances in the underlying latent variable and γ is a vector of parameters to be estimated.

14. In democratic regimes, leaders often have full control over who will compose their cabinet. In democracies, however, the cabinet is not the group that can oust the leader. Democratic leaders can appoint high-skilled individuals to the cabinet and the various executive offices charged with providing the government with expertise without fear that doing so increases the probability that they will lose the next election.

15. In addition, a Wald test reveals that the probability that all three regime target coefficients are 0 is only 2 percent ($\chi^2 = 9.20$).

16. The results also hold when we restrict the sample to just authoritarian targets: compared to single-party and military targets, the coefficient of personalist target when estimating the variance of the error term is positive and statistically significant.

17. Though some may argue that the greater error variance exhibited by personalist dictatorships is really the result of greater diversity among them, there is no reason to expect personalist dictatorships to be any more diverse than other forms of dictatorship.

18. Luke Keele and David Park (2004) argue that heteroskedastic probit models suffer from fragile identification, meaning that the joint distribution of the observed variables may not provide enough information to calculate the parameter exactly (Manski 1999). Because of this, one should estimate models both with and without controls for heteroskedasticity in order to determine whether misspecification of the variance model could be the cause of any seemingly major differences in conclusions (Williams 2006, p. 31).

19. We aggregate military and single-party dictatorships because the sample size of military targets is too small to estimate the model with the appropriate controls.

20. We exclude the control variables measuring whether states are major or minor powers due to lack of variation in the subsamples.

21. One reason that signals like audience costs might be misread, for example, is that some personalist dictators may not grasp that democratic leaders face high costs for backing down on threats when they themselves face few costs. Dictators who face no domestic accountability may not understand the extent to which other leaders do. Such misperceptions should be less pervasive when leaders are surrounded by highly skilled advisers.

22. Kristian Gleditsch and Erik Gartzke also comment on this, noting that simply using Huber-White standard errors is a "total black-box procedure, revealing nothing about the sources of unequal variances or their theoretical implications" (2007, p. 2).

23. Differences in variance can also lead to problems in statistical analyses. As Reed points out, the logit and probit models frequently employed by international politics researchers may yield inconsistent parameter estimates as a result of the heterogeneity present in international relations data (2003a, p. 68).

5

Understanding Policy Changes

Cold and distant from his ministers and supporters and having culti-
vated a reduced circle of "political counselors," [Antonio] Salazar
stamped his own style on the management of government and politics. The main characteristic of this style was an almost obsessive
concern for the minutiae of all areas of government. Despite surrounding himself with competent ministers, Salazar refused to
allow them anything but the smallest margin for autonomous decisionmaking.

—António Costa Pinto (2002, p. 432)

Comparisons of democratic versus dictatorial governance have
revealed interesting differences in the policy outcomes of
these regimes. Dictatorships tend to spend less on social programs and public goods than democracies (Brown and Hunter 1999;
Lake and Baum 2001) and they tend to pay lower wages (Przeworski
et al. 2000). Dictatorships tend to have more redistributive income
taxes than democratic regimes (Mulligan, Gil, and Sala-i-Martin
2004) and they tend to attract lower levels of foreign direct investment (FDI) inflows (Jensen 2003). Democracies and dictatorships
also differ in areas such as environmental policy. Even after controlling for level of development, democracies are more likely to sign
international conventions on the environment than dictatorships are
(Congleton 1992). There is also evidence that authoritarian governments enforce property rights more weakly than democracies (Keefer
and Knack 1997).

In recent years, there has been an increasing recognition that the
category of dictatorship masks interesting variations in the institutional structure of these regimes. Some dictatorships have legislatures,

while others do not. In some dictatorships, there is collegial leadership, while others are characterized by one-person rule. Some dictatorships hold regular, semicompetitive elections, while others ban all forms of political activity.[1] Such differences help to explain variations across dictatorships with respect to multiple items of interest, such as regime survival (Geddes 2003), economic performance (Gandhi 2008; Wright 2008), and property rights systems (Haber 2006).

Yet, who influences policies in dictatorships? Leaders obviously play a role in the direction of policy, but are all policies in dictatorships a reflection of one person's preferences? These are important questions, for foreign policy makers and investors alike. If we want to better understand the types of policies that dictatorships will pursue, it is critical that we identify the actors who influence these decisions and the extent to which they can do so.

In this chapter, we examine how institutional differences across dictatorships affect the ability of dictators to change policy. As discussed in Chapter 2, the tenure of authoritarian leaders is contingent upon the support of their elite support coalitions. Coalitions support the leader in exchange for political and economic benefits, and the leader bargains with the group to determine the price of its support. Just as prime ministers require the approval of parliament to stay in power in parliamentary regimes, leaders in dictatorships require the support of the elite coalition. Dictators must take into account the policy preferences of this group or risk being deposed.[2] Elites sustain the leader in power as long as they support the dictator's policies. We assume that all leaders prefer to remain in power and therefore seek policies that will satisfy those who can oust them. The implication is that the dictator's elite support group can essentially veto proposed policies by collectively threatening to overthrow the dictator.[3]

We show that dictators and their support coalitions can essentially be seen as veto players (Tsebelis 2002). Veto players are the political players whose consent is necessary to change policy. The number and ideological position of veto players help to explain how easy or hard it is to change policy. Governments with many ideologically dispersed veto players face greater difficulties changing the status quo than do governments with few ideologically close veto players.

We argue that institutional differences across dictatorships influence their veto player constellations and, consequently, the ease with which regimes can enact large swings in policy. Personalist dictatorships are characterized by a single veto player, the leader of the regime, while military and single-party dictatorships are characterized by two veto players, the leader of the regime (an individual veto player) and the elite coalition (a collective veto player).[4] Given such veto player arrangements, it should be easier to significantly change policy in personalist regimes and more difficult in single-party and military regimes.

Our findings largely support this prediction. The capacity of leaders to enact large policy changes varies systematically across dictatorships. Policy outcomes are more volatile in personalist dictatorships than in single-party or military dictatorships. In personalist dictatorships, large swings in policy are easier to implement and the policy environment is less predictable. By contrast, in single-party and military dictatorships, policy changes tend to be incremental and significant departures in policy more difficult to agree to. We find that it is easier for personalist dictators to respond to crises—should they choose to—than it is for single-party or military dictators. The ability to enact significant policy changes, however, has its drawbacks. We also find that due to the potential volatility of the policy environment in personalist dictatorships, these regimes are also less likely to attract foreign investment.

These findings have important implications. Large swings in policy can affect the economic performance of regimes. Indeed, volatility in policy has been shown to negatively impact long-term growth rates (Fatas and Mihov 2005, p. 3). Showing that institutional differences across dictatorships have predictable policy consequences, ranging across fundamental economic and political issues, marks an important advance over analytical approaches that do not distinguish between authoritarian regime institutional structures. Our findings suggest how greater analytical leverage for understanding policy changes in the nondemocratic world can be gained by adopting a perspective that focuses on the coalitional architecture of autocracies. This analytical gain occurs not only because these institutions matter, but also because underlying mechanisms operate widely throughout the political world. Thus, one can borrow strength from research about them that goes far beyond democratic settings.

How Authoritarianism Influences Veto Player Arrangements

We argue that governance by a party or the military institution influences the veto player arrangements of dictatorships and, consequently, the ease with which leaders can implement changes in policy. In nearly all dictatorships, the leader of the regime functions as an individual veto player. What differs across dictatorships is the role that the leader's elite support group plays in the veto player arrangement. Due to institutional differences in the composition of this group across dictatorships, in contrast to single-party and military regimes, elites in personalist regimes tend to share the same ideal preference point (i.e., similar policy goals) as the dictator.

As a broad approximation, these differences imply that personalist dictatorships consist of an individual veto player (the leader of the regime), while military and single-party dictatorships consist of two veto players, an individual veto player (the leader of the regime) and a collective veto player (the elite coalition). Given such veto player constellations, the veto players theory predicts that it should be easier to enact large policy changes in personalist regimes than in military or single-party regimes.

The key difference here is that in personalist dictatorships the elite coalition tends to share the same ideal preference point as the dictator.[5] As discussed in Chapter 2, the elite coalition in personalist dictatorships is not organized into a professional party or military, as it is in single-party and military dictatorships. As a result, members of the personalist clique are less likely to bargain with the dictator as a collective. Instead, elites tend to bargain with the dictator individually and compete with one another, driving down the price of their support (Geddes 2004). The dictator finds individuals to support him and his policy choices. Dissenters are easily replaced.

Indeed, purges of the personalist clique are quite common. In Iraq, for example, Saddam Hussein executed most members of his personalist clique in 1979 and replaced them with new supporters. Many of those executed "had been among Saddam Hussein's most intimate associates . . . even those closest to him could fall suddenly and fatally from favor" (Farouk-Sluglett and Sluglett 2001, p. 209). Out of fear of replacement, members of the clique frequently communicate to the dictator what he wants to hear, as discussed in Chapter 4.[6] In the Central African Republic, Jean-Bédel Bokassa was known to behave ruthlessly toward his aides and often sent those seen as untrustworthy to face firing squads in distant garrisons (Decalo 1985, p. 223). Purges such as these reflect the superior bargaining power of the personalist leader vis-à-vis the members of the elite coalition.

Because of this inferior bargaining position, the preferences of the elite coalition in personalist dictatorships often mirror those of the personalist dictator. Elite preferences can essentially be seen as reflections of the dictator's preferences. What does this imply for the veto player arrangement of personalist dictatorships? Additional veto players do not make policies sticky if their ideal preferences are the same as those of the existing veto players. This is referred to as the "absorption rule" (Tsebelis 2002). The preferences of elites in personalist regimes, then, are "absorbed" by those of the dictator. This implies that the elite coalition is not a de facto collective veto player in personalist regimes. Personalist dictatorships consist of one veto player: the leader of the regime. Consequently, changes in policy should be entirely determined by the preferences of the dictator.

Numerous studies have emphasized the concentration-of-power characteristic of personalist regimes (Hartlyn 1998; Farouk-Sluglett and Sluglett 2001; Decalo 1989). In Portugal, for example, the relationship between António Salazar and his ministers was "one of the concentration of decision-making power in the person of the dictator and of the reduction of the independence of both the ministers and of the president of the republic" (Costa Pinto 2002, p. 432). The political decisionmaking and implementation processes under Salazar were never challenged by independent political institutions or entities (Costa Pinto 2002, p. 437). The same is true of the Philippines under Ferdinand Marcos. The regime was characterized by highly centralized decisionmaking and Marcos "had to decide everything personally, large or small" (McVey 1992, p. 154). Similarly, in Malawi, Hastings Banda in his first decade of power was known to personally assess every application submitted for a business license (Decalo 1989, p. 272). In the Dominican Republic, Rafael Trujillo's concentration of power was extreme: "power was not shared, even among a small clique, but concentrated in the hands of one individual" (Wiarda 1968, p. 26). A whopping 60 percent of the country's labor force depended on Trujillo, directly or indirectly, with 45 percent working for his firms and 15 percent working for the state (Moya Pons 1995, p. 398). Bokassa's power in the Central African Republic was so concentrated that when he went abroad, the state fell apart because no decisions could be made without him! As Alexander Lukashenko of Belarus told a radio station in 2003: "An authoritarian ruling style is characteristic of me, and I have always admitted it. Why? We could spend hours talking about this. You need to control the country and the main thing is not to ruin people's lives" ("Europe's Last Dictatorship" 2006).

Because members of the elite coalition in personalist regimes are not bound together by a unifying organization, such as a strong party or military, personalist dictators should have a better bargaining position and select to the coalition those individuals who share their preferences. The preferences of elites should be absorbed by the dictator and policy changes should largely reflect the dictator's preferences.

It is important to note that our argument assumes that both leaders' and elites' preferences are fixed, as is traditional in the institutional analysis literature (Diermeier and Krehbiel 2003). Though the structure of personalist dictatorships makes it easier for leaders to select those individuals who share their preferences, it does not alter elite preferences. It is not that personalist dictatorship creates incentives for elites to alter their preferences to mirror those of the dictator, but rather that personalist dictatorship leads to the selection of elites who are sycophants. Personalist dictators, because they have the power to do so, will appoint to their support group those individuals who are willing to agree to whatever they say, as discussed in Chapter 4.

As shown in Chapter 2, by contrast, elites in single-party and military dictatorships are unified by membership to the dominant organization, the party and the military respectively. They bargain with the dictator as a collective, driving up the price of their support. Single-party and military elites often do not share the same policy preferences as the dictator because the dictator does not have full control over their selection. As a result, elites in single-party and military dictatorships function as a de facto collective veto player. The veto players theory predicts, then, that there should be greater capacity for significant policy changes in personalist dictatorships than in military or single-party dictatorships.

Anecdotal evidence supports this. In the Philippines under Marcos there was an "unpredictability and inconsistency in state policies as personal whims triumphed" (Haggard 1988, p. 97). Marcos had complete budgetary control and at one point 10 percent of all ministerial budgets went to his wife's "personal projects" (Montes 1988, p. 108). The reign of Bokassa, the "emperor" of the Central African Republic, provides another example of this. Between 1976 and 1977 alone, Bokassa changed the Central African Republic from a capitalist state to a socialist state to an Islamic republic to an empire. Bokassa's policy choices were often arbitrary and unpredictable (Titley 1997, p. 44), mainly due to his "excessive vanity, flights of fancy, and whimsical vacillations" (Decalo 1985, p. 225). Because personalist dictatorships essentially comprise a single veto player, changes in policy are relatively easy to realize. As Muammar Qaddafi's son Saif al-Islam said in an interview, "the moment we sat together and decided to solve the issue, we solved it in a couple of days. . . . It's very easy to reform the economy, to modernize our country" ("'A Happy Ending': Gaddafi Son Hails Nurses Accord" 2007).

In single-party and military dictatorships, by contrast, policies are less volatile. In Vietnam's single-party dictatorship, for example, gridlock is common, as elites are not always cohesive on all matters (Koh 2001). Due to internal disagreements, "economic policy muddles through the middle of the road" and the leader has no choice but to move cautiously (Koh 2001, p. 542). In the Soviet Union as well, some argue that the system failed not because the Soviet leaders did not attempt change, but because their attempts were so often defeated by institutional resistance to reform (Roeder 1993). As the need for reform continued to mount, stability became a fatal flaw. Because military and single-party dictatorships are characterized by two veto players, there is greater stability in their policy environments than in personalist dictatorships.

Institutional differences across dictatorships influence the nature of their veto player constellations. Due to these differences, policies should be more stable in single-party and military regimes than in personalist regimes.

Testing the Argument

We expect to see greater flexibility in policymaking in personalist dictatorships than in military or single-party dictatorships. The capacity for large policy changes, however, does not always mean that large policy changes will occur. As George Tsebelis writes, "It is inappropriate to conclude that because the winset of the status quo is large in a particular case, the new policy will be far away from it. The correct conclusion is that when the winset of the status quo is small, the policy adopted will be close to it" (2002, p. 32).[7] As a result, single-party and military regimes should be expected to exhibit primarily small departures in policy, whereas personalist dictatorships should be expected to exhibit both small and large departures in policy.

Due to the opacity of dictatorships, it is impossible to test how easy or hard it is to change policy in these regimes.[8] Because of this, we instead test three implications of our argument. In all of our tests, the key independent variable of interest is the type of dictatorship, which we measure again using Barbara Geddes's (2003) codings. We create dummy variables for each regime type, comparing personalist dictatorships with single-party and military dictatorships.[9] We aggregate military and single-party dictatorships because there are few military dictatorships in our samples.

The rest of the data we use come primarily from the World Bank (2003). A list of all variables and data sources is presented in Appendix B. Because data for most variables are available only from 1960 onward, we only include regimes in existence from 1960 to 2000. The dataset includes up to 64 countries and 78 regimes, with each regime representing dictatorships as coded by Geddes. Because poverty and domestic violence likely influence all of the outcomes we are interested in, we include in all of our tests a control variable for level of development (gross domestic product [GDP] per capita, logged) and a dummy variable measuring whether the country underwent a civil war during the relevant period. We also include, where noted, dummy variables measuring time period in five-year intervals. Total sample size varies in each regression due to missing data.[10]

Because it is likely that there are some unobservable factors that affect both the type of dictatorship and our dependent variables of interest, as Jennifer Gandhi (2008) has demonstrated, we present results from a Heckman selection model in every table (Heckman 1979). This model controls for possible selection effects to ensure that the estimates of regime type are not biased. As in Chapter 2, to estimate the selection-corrected effects of authoritarian regime type, we use logged GDP per capita, instance of civil war, dummy variables measuring region, and fuel exports (as a percentage of merchandise exports, logged) to generate multinomial logit estimates of the authoritarian regime type. We then use inverse Mills ratios generated from these predicted results in our models. In nearly all cases, the selection-corrected estimates are nearly identical to the uncorrected estimates.

Reactions to Exogenous Price Shocks

Our first test relates to how quickly regimes respond to exogenous price shocks. As Tsebelis writes, "Many veto players with big ideological distances between them means that legislation can only be incremental. If an exogenous shock occurs, a government with many veto players with big ideological distances among them cannot handle the situation and cannot agree on the necessary policies" (2002, p. 185). Using the same logic, it follows that dictatorships with few veto players should be better able to respond to exogenous price shocks than dictatorships with multiple veto players. In regimes where there is little constraint on executive policymaking, it should be easier to respond to dramatic changes in international prices. After a major price shock, most governments should try to reduce government expenditures (Tanzi 1986; Hunt 2002). Their capacity to do so, however, will depend on the policymaking constraints that they face. As James Poterba (1994) and James Alt and Robert Lowry (1994) show, governments that are internally divided are less reactive fiscally to changing economic conditions. Witold Henisz sums it up well: "Checks and balances on policy-makers' discretion should serve to moderate the policy response to exogenous economic shocks. Constrained policymakers will be less able to craft a change in a given policy that is amenable to all veto players and the status quo policy will be likely to persist even in the face of a substantial shift in the macroeconomic environment" (2004, p. 7). Thus, personalist dictatorships should have greater capacity to reduce spending following an exogenous price shock than military or single-party dictatorships.

To test this implication, we analyze regime reactions to the 1973 and 1979 oil crises. In response to a sharp rise in oil prices, governments should try to reduce government spending (Tanzi 1986; Hunt 2002). We gathered data on government expenditure for the year preceding and the year following each of the shocks and calculated the difference between the two (as a percentage of GDP). A positive value for this variable, reduction in expenditure, indicates that the regime reduced expenditure in response to the shock. The number of regimes included in these samples is obviously restricted to those in existence during the time of the shocks. Because of this, there are only 52 observations. We include a dummy variable for the year of the first shock to control for the possibility that reactions differed in magnitude from one shock to the next.

The capacity to change policy does not always mean that it will be changed, however, as noted previously. How dramatically policy is altered from one year to the next will depend on the exact preferences of the players. Because of the large size of the winset of the status quo, for example, personalist dictators may or may not elect to reduce spending, depending on their preferences. This means that we should also expect there to be decreasing variance in the reduction of spending as the number and distance between veto players increase. Personalist dictatorships should have higher variance in their responses to shocks than single-party or military regimes.

Due to the nature of these predictions, we use a statistical model that estimates both relationships simultaneously, called multiplicative heteroskedastic regression (Harvey 1976; Greene 2000).[11] By using this model, heteroskedastic residuals do not affect the statistical significance of coefficients. Multiplicative heteroskedastic regression incorporates both a test of means (regression) and a test of heteroskedastic residuals. With this model, the following equations can be estimated at the same time using maximum-likelihood estimation:

$$\text{Reduction in expenditure} = \alpha_1 + \beta_1 \text{ (Personalist)} + \varepsilon_1 \qquad (1)$$
$$\text{Var}(\varepsilon_1) = \exp\left[\alpha_2 + \beta_2 \text{ (Personalist)}\right] \qquad (2)$$

We expect personalist dictatorships will have a positive coefficient when estimating the mean and when estimating the variance of the error term. As Tsebelis points out, "If the data support both relationships, then the confidence in the theory that predicted them should be significantly higher than the p-value of any one coefficient" (2002, p. 172).

In addition to controls for GDP capita and civil war, we include fuel exports to account for the possibility that oil-producing countries actually benefit from the oil shock, and a measure of prior expenditure (as a percentage of GDP) during the year prior to the shock. Regimes with high expenditure levels prior to the shock may reduce expenditure proportionately following the shock. We also use Huber-White standard errors to take into account the fact that a regime's reaction to the first shock is not independent from its reaction to the second shock.[12] The regression results are presented in Table 5.1.[13]

As Model 2 shows, personalist dictatorships on average reduce expenditure by about 3 percent more than do single-party and military dictatorships (as a percentage of GDP). Given that the interquartile range of reduction in expenditure is 4.4 percent, the difference between single-party and military dictatorships and personalist dictatorships is fairly large in substantive terms. The coefficient of personalist dictatorship is also statistically significant at the .05 level.

With respect to the heteroskedasticity tests, the coefficient of per-

Table 5.1   Reduction in Expenditure Following Exogenous Price Shock

	Model 1	Model 2 (selection model)
Dependent variable: reduction in expenditure (percentage of GDP)		
Personalist dictatorships	3.4*	3.2**
	(1.88)	(1.64)
Civil war	.81	.39
	(.29)	(.86)
GDP per capita (logged)	.78	–3.0**
	(1.0)	(1.5)
Fuel exports (percentage of merchandise exports) (logged)	.13	.57*
	(.32)	(.34)
Prior expenditure (percentage of GDP) (logged)	9.3***	12.29***
	(3.5)	(3.5)
Constant	–16.6***	–7.01
	(6.41)	(5.0)
N	52	52
Countries	36	36
Dependent variable: variance of error term of reduction in expenditure (percentage of GDP)		
Personalist dictatorships	1.65***	2.15***
	(.67)	(.65)
Constant	2.02***	1.89***
	(.33)	(.33)
Chi^2	51.5	57.9
$(P > chi^2)$	(.000)	(.000)
Likelihood ratio test		$P > chi^2 = .006$

Notes: Estimation is by multiplicative heteroskedastic regression; Huber-White standard errors (clustered by country) are in parentheses. Each regression also includes a dummy for the year of the first shock; coefficients on this variable (not reported) are available upon request. * $p < .10$, ** $p < .05$, *** $p < .01$; two-tailed tests.

sonalist dictatorships is positive and statistically significant, indicating that there is more variance in the residuals among personalist dictatorships. Personalist dictatorships exhibit greater variation in the reduction of expenditure than single-party and military dictatorships, as predicted.

The results of the tests of this implication confirm our expectations. Single-party and military regimes are less able than personalist regimes to reduce spending in response to exogenous price shocks. There is also more variance in responses to the shocks among personalist dictatorships compared to military and single-party regimes. These findings reflect that it is easier for personalist dictators to implement dramatic changes in policy and more difficult for military and single-party dictators.

Control over Inflationary Policy

Our second test focuses on the stability of inflation rates. Daniel Treisman (2000) shows that countries that are more decentralized have steadier average inflation rates, whether high or low. This is because the federal structure locks in existing patterns of monetary policy, whether strict or inflationary. While not synonymous, federalism implies multiple veto players. Though the argument does not perfectly apply to dictatorships, it should hold due to the varying level of constraints on the executive among dictatorships with respect to policy implementation. Therefore we should expect to see stable inflation rates from year to year (whether high or low) among single-party and military regimes, and fluctuations in inflation rates from year to year among personalist regimes.

We test this implication in two different ways. The first is by looking at annual variations in inflation rates in each regime. As the size and dispersion of veto players increase, inflation rates, whether low or high, should vary little from one year to the next. The inflation rates of personalist dictatorships should vary more from year to year than the inflation rates of single-party or military dictatorships. To test this, we calculate the standard deviation of inflation in the second through sixth years of each regime. Because there are substantial differences in the durations of regimes, we use a five-year block of time near the beginning of each regime and exclude the first year of the regime so that monetary problems associated with the start of the regime do not affect our results. We log this variable to avoid giving too much weight to cases of hyperinflation, which is widely thought to be generated by a nonlinear process.

Because the ability to enact large policy changes does not always mean that they will occur, as discussed previously, we also test for heteroskedasticity. As the number and distance between veto players increase, we should see a decrease in variance in the fluctuation of inflation rates. For this reason, we test whether there is higher variance in the fluctuation of inflation rates among personalist dictatorships than among other forms of dictatorships. We expect that the coefficient for personalist dictatorships will be positive when estimating the mean of the standard deviation of inflation and when estimating the variance of the error term.

A number of additional controls are included as well. The first is the standard deviation of prior world inflation rates (logged) for the relevant period, excluding the regime in question. This variable accounts for worldwide economic fluctuations that may affect individual regimes. The inflation rate of the first year of the regime, prior inflation (logged), is also included to control for the possibility that prior inflation rates affect the inflation rates of the years that follow. Last, a measure of imports (as a percentage of GDP) is included to take into account that higher exposure to imports might reduce inflation (Romer 1993).[14]

Because some countries have experienced multiple dictatorships, Huber-White robust standard errors were calculated to account for the possibility that regimes occurring within the same country are not independent. The results are presented in Table 5.2.

As the table reveals, the results support our argument. In Model 4, personalist dictatorships have an average standard deviation of inflation (unlogged) that is .86 percent higher than in single-party and military dictatorships.[15] Given that the range of standard deviation of inflation in the entire sample is 2 percent, these are substantively notable differences. The coefficients of both regime variables are also statistically significant at the .01 level.

The results of the heteroskedasticity test also support our argument. The personalist coefficient is positive and statistically significant at the .01 level. This indicates that the variance of the error term is largest among personalist regimes, as predicted.

We also test this implication using time-series cross-sectional data, and essentially replicate Daniel Treisman's (2000) tests, by looking at the effect of past inflation on future inflation, given regime type. We expect that in regimes with multiple, dispersed veto players, there should be continuity in inflation, whether high or low. This means that inflation for single-party and military regimes should be lower than inflation for personalist regimes, given low levels of previous inflation, but higher than inflation for personalist regimes, given high levels of previous inflation. To test this, we follow

Table 5.2   Fluctuations in Inflation

	Model 3	Model 4 (selection model)
Dependent variable: *standard deviation of inflation (logged)*		
Personalist dictatorships	.27**	.27**
	(.14)	(.13)
Prior inflation (logged)	.37***	.37***
	(.13)	(.14)
Civil war	−.08	−.08
	(.14)	(.15)
GDP per capita (logged)	−.09	−.06
	(.14)	(.15)
Imports (percentage of GDP)	−.01***	−.01**
	(.003)	(.003)
Standard deviation of prior world inflation (logged)	−.19	−.19
	(.18)	(.18)
Constant	.67	.68
	(.49)	(1.02)
N	43	43
Countries	37	37
Dependent variable: *variance of error term of* *standard deviation of inflation (logged)*		
Personalist dictatorships	1.6***	1.6***
	(.58)	(.58)
Constant	−3.03***	−3.03***
	(.34)	(.34)
Chi^2	38.30	38.3
$(P > chi^2)$	(.000)	(.000)
Likelihood ratio test		$P > chi^2 = .0001$

Notes: Estimation is by multiplicative heteroskedastic regression; Huber-White standard errors (clustered by country) are in parentheses. Each regression also includes dummy variables for time period and region. Coefficients on these (not reported) are available upon request. * $p < .10$, ** $p < .05$, *** $p < .01$; two-tailed tests.

Treisman (2000) and analyze the relationship between annual rates of lagged inflation (from the previous year, logged) and current inflation (logged) among each regime type using interaction terms.

The correlation between lagged inflation and inflation should be strongest in single-party and military dictatorships and weakest in personalist dictatorships. Indeed, the correlation is .88 in single-party dictatorships, .84 in military dictatorships, and .75 in personalist dictatorships. In our regressions, we expect that the coefficient of the personalist interaction will be negative and the coefficient of personalist dictatorships will be positive.[16]

For the same reasons as already mentioned, we also test for heteroskedasticity by using multiplicative heteroskedastic regression. We expect the coefficient of personalist dictatorships to be positive when estimating the variance of the error term. Since visual examinations of the data indicate that the variance of inflation increases markedly as lagged inflation increases, we also include lagged inflation as a predictor of the variance of the error term.

Because our model includes a lagged dependent variable, we include fixed effects with robust standard errors in order to correct for panel heteroskedasticity and contemporaneous correlation of the errors. Sven Wilson and Daniel Butler (2007) show that fixed effects with robust standard errors should be used when lagged dependent variables are included in models that have a correlation between unit effects and the explanatory variables.[17] One problem with including fixed effects, however, is that the independent variable of interest, regime type, does not typically change much from one year to the next. Fixed effects can make it difficult to show that slow-moving, time-invariant variables actually have an effect. We also tested our model excluding the fixed effects and found the results to be nearly identical.

We include virtually all the same controls as in the previous test, except that we do not use the standard deviation of prior world inflation, but rather lagged world inflation excluding the regime in question (prior world inflation, logged).[18] Because Treisman includes a measure of the number of years of democracy, we include a measure of the number of years the dictatorship has been in power (years authoritarian, logged). We also include an interaction between civil war and lagged inflation because it is possible that the relationship between prior inflation and future inflation is different in countries experiencing civil war. All control variables are lagged one year to avoid endogeneity problems. The results are presented in Table 5.3.

As the table indicates, the results as a whole confirm our expectations. The coefficient of personalist dictatorships is positive and statistically significant at the .01 level. In addition, the coefficient of the personalist interaction is negative and statistically significant at the .01 level. The magnitude of these effects is displayed in Figure 5.1. At low levels of prior inflation, personalist dictatorships have higher inflation than military and single-party dictatorships. At high levels

Table 5.3   Time-Series Cross-Sectional Tests of Inflation

	Model 5	Model 6	Model 7 (selection model)
Dependent variable: annual inflation (logged)			
Personalist dictatorships	1.14***	1.51 ***	1.48***
	(.27)	(.30)	(.30)
Lagged inflation (logged)	.60***	.57***	.57***
	(.05)	(.05)	(.05)
Personalist interaction	.37***	.47***	.47***
	(.08)	(.09)	(.09)
Civil war	—	–.62**	.65**
		(.29)	(.29)
Civil war interaction	—	.23**	.23***
		(.09)	(.09)
GDP per capita (logged)	—	–.25***	.43***
		(.08)	(.15)
Imports (percentage of GDP)	—	.003***	.003***
		(.001)	(.001)
Prior world inflation (logged)	—	.07*	.07*
		(.04)	(.08)
Years authoritarian (logged)	—	.07***	.07***
		(.03)	(.02)
Constant	.49***	1.6***	2.2***
	(.48)	(.27)	(.56)
N	1,030	1,030	1,030
Countries	64	64	64
Dependent variable: variance of error term of inflation (logged)			
Personalist dictatorships	.91***	.87***	.86***
	(.23)	(.23)	(.22)
Lagged inflation (logged)	.74***	.70***	.70***
	(.13)	(.11)	(.11)
Constant	–4.9***	–4.9***	–4.9***
	(.48)	(.41)	(.41)
Chi^2	1,725	1,765	1,766
(P > chi^2)	(.000)	(.000)	(.000)
Likelihood ratio test			P > chi^2 = .0001

Notes: Estimation is by multiplicative heteroskedastic regression with fixed effects; robust standard errors are in parentheses. Each regression also includes dummy variables for time period. Coefficients on these (not reported) are available upon request. "—" indicates not applicable. * p < .10, ** p < .05, *** p < .01; two-tailed tests.

Figure 5.1 Inflation and Veto Players (percentage)

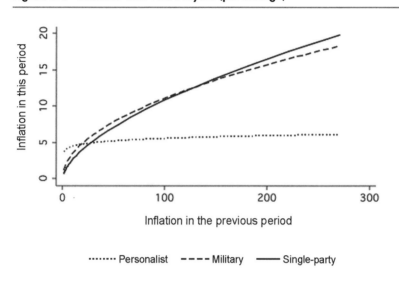

Inflation in the previous period

········ Personalist   ⎯ ⎯ ⎯ Military   ⎯⎯⎯ Single-party

of prior inflation, military and single-party dictatorships have higher inflation than personalist dictatorships. The graph indicates that, among dictatorships, there is considerably less continuity in inflation, whether high or low, in personalist dictatorships.

The heteroskedasticity tests are also supportive: personalist dictatorships exhibit greater variance in inflation compared to military and single-party dictatorships. This effect is also statistically significant, at the .01 level.

The results of these tests indicate that there is a greater continuity in inflation, whether high or low, among single-party and military dictatorships. Single-party and military regimes have the steadiest inflation patterns, while inflation in personalist regimes varies markedly from one year to the next. Because it is more difficult to change policy in single-party and military dictatorships than in personalist dictatorships, existing patterns of monetary policy in these regimes become locked-in.

Foreign Direct Investment

We next test how well dictatorships are able to attract foreign direct investment. Nathan Jensen (2003) shows that democratic political

institutions are associated with higher levels of FDI inflows. He finds
that this is the case because democratic institutions are associated with
lower levels of political risk. He writes, "Democratic institutions
decrease the political risks of government leaders choosing policies
that negatively affect multinational operations, leading to higher levels
of FDI" (Jensen 2003, p. 609). Greater stability in policy should lead
to higher levels of FDI inflows; the presence of multiple, dispersed
veto players should increase the predictability of the political context
in which multinationals operate. Recent empirical analyses largely
support this view (Bergara, Henisz, and Spiller 1997; Henisz 2000).

  Therefore, personalist dictatorships should have lower levels of FDI
than military or single-party dictatorships. In Belarus under Lukashenko,
for example, scholars found it surprising that FDI was low, even though
Belarus "is linked to markets in Russia which may be promising to market seeking foreign investors" (Budrauskaite et al. 2002, p. 89). The
same is true of the Philippines under Marcos. In comparison to the
Philippines, the military dictatorship in Thailand attracted "a huge surge
of FDI inflows in the 1980s" (Kind 2000, p. 30). While neighboring
Malaysia and Singapore, both single-party dictatorships, attracted high
levels of FDI, "towards the end of Marcos' regime both net and gross
FDI to the Philippines were close to zero" (Kind 2000, p. 29).

  We test this expectation that personalist dictatorships should
attract lower levels of FDI compared to other forms of dictatorship by
looking at annual net FDI inflows as a percentage of GDP, from 1960
to 2000. This variable is logged to normalize its distribution. We
exclude the first year of each regime and lag all control variables one
year to avoid problems of endogeneity. In addition to controls for
GDP per capita, civil war, and fuel exports, following Jensen (2003)
we also include measures of government consumption (as a percentage of GDP, logged), market size (the log of GDP), trade (measured
as exports plus imports divided by GDP), growth, and a dummy variable measuring whether or not there are FDI inflows controls.[19] In
addition, we include lagged FDI, logged.

  To estimate this relationship, we use ordinary least squares
regression with fixed effects and robust standard errors. We expect
the coefficient of personalist dictatorships to be negative. The results
are presented in Table 5.4.

  Our expectations are largely supported by the data. In Model 10,
the coefficient of personalist dictatorships is negative and statistically
significant. Substantively, holding all other variables at their means,

Table 5.4   Time-Series Cross-Sectional Tests of Foreign Direct Investment

Dependent Variable: Annual Net FDI Inflows (percentage of GDP) (logged)	Model 8	Model 9	Model 10 (selection model)
Personalist dictatorships	−.98***	−.70**	−.70**
	(.30)	(.36)	(.37)
Government consumption (percentage of GDP) (logged)	—	.15	.15
		(.26)	(.28)
GDP per capita (logged)	—	−1.5*	−1.45
		(.97)	(1.03)
Market size (logged)	—	.95	.92
		(.93)	(.98)
Growth	—	.03**	.02**
		(.01)	(.01)
Lagged FDI (logged)	—	.32***	.32***
		(.06)	(.06)
FDI inflows controls	—	−.56**	−.55**
		(.27)	(.27)
Trade	—	.01***	.01***
		(.003)	(.004)
Civil war	—	−.83**	−.75
		(.40)	(.63)
Fuel exports (percentage of merchandise exports) (logged)	—	.005	−.02
		(.04)	(.10)
Constant	−.20	−12.7	−12.3
	(.18)	(15)	(14.8)
N	907	377	377
Countries	62	49	49
R^2	.11	.3	.3
Likelihood ratio test			$P > chi^2 = .009$

Notes: Estimation is by ordinary least squares regression with dummy variables and fixed effects; robust standard errors are in parentheses. Each regression also includes dummy variables for time period. Coefficients on these (not reported) are available upon request. "—" indicates not applicable. * p < .10, ** p < .05, *** p < .01; two-tailed tests.

net FDI inflows (unlogged) in single-party and military dictatorships are about .7 percent higher than they are in personalist dictatorships. Given that the average of net FDI inflows is .8 percent in personalist dictatorships, these are substantively large differences. Foreign direct investment inflows are greater in single-party and military regimes than in personalist regimes.[20]

This is a reflection of the greater predictability of the policy environment in single-party and military dictatorships. Because it is more difficult for elites and leaders in single-party and military dictatorships to agree to large changes in policy, there are fewer swings in policy choices. The opposite is true of personalist dictatorships.

Conclusion

In this chapter we have explored how institutional differences across dictatorships shape the nature of elite-leader relations and influence how easy or hard it is for these regimes to enact significant policy changes. Using the veto players theory as a frame, with personalist dictatorships characterized by a single veto player and military and single-party dictatorships characterized by two veto players, we find substantial support for our argument that personalist regimes, in contrast to other forms of dictatorship, are more capable of implementing sizable swings in policy and tend to be characterized by a relatively unpredictable policy environment.

The insights presented in this chapter help to erode the black box that often characterizes decisionmaking in dictatorships. Policies in dictatorships typically result from bargaining between two key actors: leaders and elites. Dictators must factor in the policy preferences of their elite supporters when making policy choices, or risk being deposed.

Our findings underscore the importance of disaggregating the category of dictatorship for understanding domestic policy outcomes. Indeed, as Karen Remmer has pointed out, once the "enormous range of variation concealed within the authoritarian (and democratic) categor(ies)" is recognized, political outcomes do vary with regime type (1986, p. 68). Dictatorships differ from one another in important ways; these differences have profound implications for the ability of dictators to enact changes in policy and affect the size of these changes from one year to the next.

Notes

1. For analyses of the role and consequences of elections in authoritarian regimes, see Gandhi and Lust-Okar 2009, Blaydes 2006, and Magaloni 2006.

2. This is not to say that elites do not play a policymaking role beyond

vetoing the dictator's proposals. In many dictatorships, elites are active participants in the development of policy. The formulation of policy, however, is distinct from the ability to veto proposed policies.

3. We assume that the elite coalition can veto proposed changes only if they behave as a unitary actor. "Vetoes" should require the support of most, if not all, of the elites in the coalition. This assumption is supported by Robert Barros's (2002) finding that the Chilean military junta required unanimity to make decisions. In Vietnam, as well, "the decision rule is that no decision is to be made that is not at least tolerable to all Politburo members" (Pike 1989, p. 119).

4. Veto players can be either individual (like a president) or collective (like a senate body).

5. Additional veto players only influence policy outcomes if they hold policy preferences different from those of existing veto players.

6. For a theoretical analysis of this dynamic, see Wintrobe 1998.

7. It is for this reason that a lack of major policy changes in personalist dictatorships should not be viewed as a sign that elites have been able to overcome coordination barriers and contest the dictator's proposed policies; if the personalist dictator supports the status quo, there is simply no reason to change policy.

8. Tsebelis (2002) measures the stability of policy, for example, by looking at the number of significant legislation passed. Such data are not available for most dictatorships.

9. There are 30 personalist dictatorships, 28 single-party dictatorships, and 20 military dictatorships in our sample.

10. Because there are no data available on any indicators for many regimes, imputing the missing data was not a viable option.

11. This is the same model that Tsebelis (2002) uses to test the veto players theory. This technique allows simultaneous estimation of the expected value and the variance of the dependent variable using maximum-likelihood methods.

12. Huber-White standard errors were generated by using the "cluster" option in STATA 9 to group regimes within the same country.

13. The likelihood ratio test included in Table 5.1 (and the tables that follow) is a test of the model including the key independent variable of interest (personalist dictatorship) and the restricted model that excludes these variables.

14. Treisman (2000) also controls for central bank independence and whether countries use a fixed or pegged exchange rate. We do not control for these variables because there are very little data on central bank independence for dictatorships and because nearly every country in our sample used a pegged exchange rate.

15. Though the term "average" will be used, the coefficient derived for the dummy variables, when those variables are independent and the dependent variable is logged, is actually the median rather than the mean. The method for interpreting the logged coefficients is: $[(\log \text{base})^b] - 1$ (Halvorsen and Palmquist 1980).

16. To reiterate, at low levels of previous inflation, inflation should be

highest in personalist dictatorships; at high levels of previous inflation, inflation should be lowest in personalist dictatorships.

17. An f-test also shows that fixed effects (as opposed to random
effects) should be used.

18. As Treisman points out, the inclusion of such a measure should also
correct for contemporaneous correlation (2000, p. 840).

19. Jensen (2003) also includes a control for budget deficits. Data for
this variable are missing, however, for most countries in our dataset.

20. These results also hold when controlling for whether the country
has a legislature. Results from this model can be obtained upon request.

6

The Consequences
of Authoritarianism

Dictators are rulers who always look good until the last ten minutes.

　　　　　　　　　　　—Jan Masaryk (Kendall 2006, p. 140)

In ancient Rome, military emergencies often made unity of command desirable. The Romans' solution to this problem was the appointment of a dictator in place of the consuls. Though the motivation behind the installation of dictators may no longer remain the same, authoritarian rule is by no means a relic of the Roman era. In fact, nearly one-third of the world's countries are run by dictators. Yet, in comparison to democratic systems, many aspects of authoritarian political systems remain poorly understood.

In this study we have shown how authoritarianism shapes political outcomes. In dictatorships, most political outcomes result from a struggle for power between two actors: leaders and elites. Elites matter because they can control the fates of dictators, as most dictators are ousted by members of their own inner circle. Both actors behave in ways that will ensure their continued political influence. This struggle for power forms the core of authoritarian politics.

The institutional makeup of dictatorships affects the nature of this relationship. In particular, how dictatorships are governed, whether by a professionalized military, a political party, or neither, profoundly impacts elite politics and the dynamics of leader-elite relations. Understanding how this internal architecture of dictatorships influences the nature of the interplay between dictators and their elite supporters and, in turn, a host of political outcomes, can help inform how we think about authoritarian government.

The theoretical arguments proposed throughout this study emphasize two key dimensions, each of which impacts how power is distributed between leaders and elites. The first is whether elites share membership in a unifying institution (central to Chapters 2, 3, 4, and 5). Membership in a unifying institution, like a party or military, enables elites to bargain with the dictator as a collective. This eases coordination barriers among elites and increases their bargaining power relative to the dictator, in turn making it more difficult for dictators to appoint and dismiss coalition members at will. The second dimension is whether elites have control over the security forces (central to Chapters 2 and 3). Control over the security forces gives elites access to troops and weaponry, increasing their ability to carry out a coup and unseat the dictator.

In Chapter 2 we explored how the institutional structure of dictatorships influences one of the central aspects of authoritarian politics: leadership survival. Because authoritarianism affects the ease with which elites can unseat dictators, we argue that among the authoritarian regime types, military dictatorships face the highest risk of being overthrown by their support group, both because elites control arms and troops and also because the organization of the military lowers barriers of coordination. In single-party dictatorships, the party organization lowers the barriers of coordination but does not give members of the support group control over the resources required to overthrow the leader by force. In personalist dictatorships, by contrast, leaders have greater control in the selection of individuals to their support group and can choose those who are least likely to threaten their continued rule. Their supporters are not organized into a preexisting structure that can help to overcome coordination problems, and they often compete with one another for the leader's favor. As a result, personalist dictators face few credible threats of overthrow.

Our empirical tests indicate that the tenure of dictators is strongly influenced by the internal makeup of the regimes they rule. Military dictators face the greatest risk of being overthrown in any given year and only rule on average for around three years; followed by single-party dictators, who rule on average for around nine years; and followed last by personalist dictators, who rule on average for around ten years. Lower coordination barriers and access to troops and weaponry give military-based coalitions greater ability to depose dictators, followed by party-based coalitions, and lastly personalist coalitions.

In Chapter 3 we examined how the internal makeup of dictatorships influences whether they are likely to be participants in escalatory cross-border conflicts. Given our findings in Chapter 2, we expected that it should be easier for military elites to sanction leaders for poor foreign policy choices, followed by party elites, and lastly personalist elites. Military dictators should be better able to establish a "hands-tying" mechanism and signal their resolve during interstate disputes. The opposite should be true of personalist dictators, due to the inability to credibly signal their intentions. Our empirical tests support this expectation. Military conflict is most likely to increase in intensity when personalist dictators provoke it, followed by single-party dictators, and lastly military dictators.

In Chapter 4 we challenged the assumption that all states are equally capable of gauging the resolve of their adversaries, by looking at how the institutional structure of dictatorships influences the quality of the information channels that exist between elites and dictators. We showed that governance by a military or party not only provides elites with better incentives to relay accurate information to dictators, but also provides dictators with better incentives to select to their support group those individuals more likely to do so. As a result, personalist dictators are more likely to receive lower-quality military intelligence from their advisers in the elite coalition compared to military and single-party dictators. Poor intelligence should increase the likelihood that signals will be misread. Indeed, we find that personalist dictatorships exhibit more heterogeneity in their "reading" of signals during disputes than do other regimes. The behavior of personalist dictatorships from one conflict to the next is more erratic than that of other regimes. When targeted, personalist dictatorships are more likely to make foreign policy mistakes than are other forms of dictatorships.

In Chapter 5 we examined the impact of differences in the institutional structure of dictatorships on domestic policies, particularly the ease or difficulty that dictators face when enacting large policy changes at home. Because personalist dictators have greater control over the selection of individuals to their elite support group, they choose individuals who share their preferences, ensuring that there are no potential "vetoes" on their policies. In military and single-party dictatorships, selection to the elite coalition is largely determined by the rules for promotion as dictated by the military and the party, respectively. Dictators cannot ensure that elites will share their policy preferences, and elites can veto proposed policies by threatening to oust dictators.

We find multiple indications that this argument is true: it is more difficult to enact big policy changes in single-party regimes and military regimes than in personalist regimes. Personalist dictatorships are more capable of reducing spending following an exogenous price shock than are single-party and military dictatorships. Inflation rates are also more likely to fluctuate from year to year in personalist regimes than in other forms of dictatorship. Last, personalist dictatorships are the least capable of providing the stable policy environment desired by investors; among dictatorships, foreign direct investment is lowest in personalist regimes. Our findings demonstrate that variations in the internal makeup of dictatorships have predictable policy consequences.

Government by a party or the military as an institution has an important influence on the nature of leader-elite relations and, in turn, authoritarian politics. The theoretical mechanisms that we emphasize yield testable implications that help to explain multiple domestic and international political outcomes across dictatorships, ranging from their propensity to engage in escalatory interstate conflicts to the stability of their monetary policy. Our central conclusions have implications for how we think about authoritarian politics, as well as for future discussions of the pros and cons of authoritarianism. While some dictatorships behave in ways easily identified as "authoritarian," others exhibit much more "democratic" behavior than we might expect.

As this study has demonstrated, a variety of extant theories in both economics and political science can inform our understanding of politics in the authoritarian world. With some tinkering, theories of labor unions can give us insights into the role of military and party organizations in dictatorships, theories of the democratic peace can lend themselves to an understanding of the role of autocratic institutions in conflict behavior, and theories of policymaking in democracies can translate well to the policymaking processes of autocracies. It is true that authoritarian regimes are difficult regimes to study: the internal political process is hidden, government propaganda is widespread, and the media are censored. There are indeed accessible ways, however, in which we can theorize and generate expectations about how dictatorships work, an endeavor that, given the persistence of this form of government, remains as essential as ever.

Appendix A:
Explanation of Variables in Chapter 2

Ouster by Insiders

This variable is coded 1 if members of the military, elites, or their allies are responsible for the removal of the dictator, and coded 0 otherwise. We automatically code this variable 1 if the leader is ousted but the regime does not collapse. The assumption is that, given that the regime continued, elites must have approved the transfer of power. If the leader is ousted and the regime collapses, we examine each case individually to determine whether a regime insider was responsible for the leader's downfall. Individuals are considered to be regime insiders if they are close friends, advisers, or family members of the dictator, if they hold key executive positions of power (e.g., cabinet members), or if they are high-ranking members of the military. Estranged family members, junior officers in the military, officers from disfavored tribes, and high-ranking members of the military who are part of a rival faction within the military are not considered to be insiders, unless there are indications that they colluded with high-ranking elites in removing the dictator. The following are cases in which regime insiders were responsible for the downfall of the dictator and the regime collapsed:

Algeria (1999)   Central African Republic (1966)
Bangladesh (1982)   Chad (1979)
Bolivia (1964)   Dominican Republic (1961)
Burkina Faso (1980, 1987)   Guatemala (1958)
Cameroon (1982)   Guinea-Bissau (1980)

Indonesia (1965)   Paraguay (1954)
Iraq (1968)   Rwanda (1973)
Mauritania (1978)   South Vietnam (1963)
Niger (1999)   Sudan (1985)
Pakistan (1969, 1977)   Uganda (1971)

Insider Succession

This variable is coded 1 if a member of the regime elite (whether part of the military or otherwise) rules following the ouster of the dictator, and coded 0 otherwise. We automatically code this variable 1 if the leader is ousted (or dies) but the regime does not collapse. The assumption is that the survival of the regime indicates successful elite transfer of power. If the leader is ousted (or dies) and the regime collapses, we examine each case individually to determine whether a regime insider rules subsequently, regardless of the duration of the successor's tenure. Individuals are considered to be regime insiders if they are close friends, advisers, or family members of the dictator, if they hold key executive positions of power (e.g., cabinet members), or if they are high-ranking members of the military. Estranged family members, junior officers in the military, officers from disfavored tribes, and high-ranking members of the military who are part of a rival faction within the military are not considered to be insiders. The following are cases in which regime insiders have ruled following the collapse of the regime (even if momentarily):

Algeria (1999)   Mauritania (1978)
Bangladesh (1982)   Niger (1999)
Bolivia (1964, 1969)   Pakistan (1969, 1977)
Burkina Faso (1980, 1987)   Paraguay (1954)
Cameroon (1982)   Rwanda (1973)
Central African Republic (1966)   South Vietnam (1963)
Guinea-Bissau (1980)   Sudan (1985)
Indonesia (1965)   Uganda (1971)
Iraq (1968)

Appendix B:
Explanation of Variables in Chapter 5

Civil war	Dummy variable coding whether the country experienced civil war (Fearon and Laitin 2003)
Fuel exports	Fuel exports as percentage of merchandise exports
GDP per capita	Purchasing power party (PPP) in international currency
Government consumption	Government consumption as percentage of GDP
Growth	Annual growth in GDP per capita
Imports	Imports as percentage of GDP
Inflation	Annual percentage inflation in consumer prices
Lagged FDI	Annual net FDI inflows as percentage of GDP in the prior year
Market size	Log of GDP
Net FDI inflows	Annual net FDI inflows as percentage of GDP
Personalist, military, single-party	Dummy variables coding regime type (hybrid regimes are not included in the dataset) (Geddes 2003)

Prior expenditure	Expenditure (current and capital) as percentage of GDP in the year prior to the price shock
Prior world inflation	World annual percentage inflation (excluding the country in question) in consumer prices, lagged one year
Reduction in expenditure	Difference between expenditure (current and capital) as percentage of GDP from the year preceding the price shock to the year following the shock; positive value indicates reduction in expenditure (regimes with no reported expenditure are excluded from this sample)
Standard deviation of inflation	Standard deviation of annual percentage inflation in consumer prices for the second through sixth years of each regime (first year of the regime is excluded from this calculation; for four regimes, we used the third through seventh years to increase the sample size)
Standard deviation of prior world inflation	Standard deviation of world annual percentage inflation (excluding the country in question) in consumer prices, lagged one year
Trade	Exports plus imports divided by GDP

Note: Source is World Bank 2003 unless otherwise noted.

References

Acemoglu, Daron, and James Robinson. 2001. "A Theory of Political Transitions." *American Economic Review* 91 (4): 938–963.

Acemoglu, Daron, James Robinson, and Thierry Verdier. 2004. "Kleptocracy and Divide and Rule: A Model of Personal Rule." *Journal of European Economic Association* 2 (3): 162–192.

Achen, Christopher H. 2002. "Toward a New Political Methodology: Microfoundations and Art." *Annual Review of Political Science* 5: 423–450.

"Adam Przeworski: Capitalism, Democracy, and Science." 2003. Interview by Gerardo L. Munck. www.nyu.edu/gsas/dept/politics/faculty/przeworski/przeworski_munck.pdf (accessed April 22, 2008).

Afoaku, Osita G. 1999. "The Politics of Democratic Transition in Congo (Zaire): Implications of the Kabila Revolution." *Journal of Conflict Studies* 19 (2): 1–21.

Albrecht, Holger, and Oliver Schlumberger. 2004. "'Waiting for Godot': Regime Change Without Democratization in the Middle East." *International Political Science Review* 25 (4): 371–392.

al-Marashi, Ibrahim. 2002. "Iraq's Security and Intelligence Network: A Guide and Analysis." *MERIA* 6 (3): 1–13.

Alt, James, and Robert Lowry. 1994. "Divided Governments, Fiscal Institutions, and Budget Deficits: Evidence for the States." *American Political Science Review* 88 (4): 811–828.

Alvarez, R. Michael, and John Brehm. 1995. "American Ambivalence Towards Abortion Policy: Development of a Heteroskedastic Probit Model of Competing Values." *American Journal of Political Science* 39 (4): 1055–1082.

Andrew, Christopher, and Julie Elkner. 2003. "Stalin and Foreign Intelligence." *Totalitarian Movements and Political Religions* 4 (1): 69–94.

Anugwom, Edlyne E. 2001. "The Military, Ethnicity, and Democracy in Nigeria." *Journal of Social Development in Africa* 16 (2): 93–114.

Arendt, Hannah. 1951. *The Origins of Totalitarianism.* New York: Harvest.

"Armistice or Peace?" 1937. *The Evening Standard,* November 11.

"Background Note: Ghana." 2008. US Department of State, June. www.state.gov/r/pa/ei/bgn/2860.htm (accessed December 23, 2008).

Banks, A. S. 2001. *Cross-National Time-Series Data Archive.* Dataset. Binghamton, NY: Computer Systems Unlimited.

Barros, Robert. 2002. *Constitutionalism and Dictatorship: Pinochet, the Junta, and the 1980 Constitution.* Cambridge: Cambridge University Press.

Basajabka, Abu, Kawalya Kasozi, Nakanyike Musis, and James Mukooza Sejjengo. 1994. *Social Origins of Violence in Uganda,1964–85.* Montreal: McGill-Queens University Press.

Baum, Matthew A. 2004a. "Going Private: Public Opinion, Presidential Rhetoric, and the Domestic Politics of Audience Costs in US Foreign Policy Crises." *Journal of Conflict Resolution* 48 (5): 603–631.

Baum, Matthew A. 2004b. "How Public Opinion Constrains the Use of Force: The Case of Operation Restore Hope." *Presidential Studies Quarterly* 24 (2): 187–226.

Beeston, Richard. 2004. "Secret Files Show Saddam Deluded to the Very End." *The Times,* March 18.

Bennett, D. Scott, and Allan Stam. 2000. "EUGene: A Conceptual Manual." *International Interactions* 26: 179–204.

Bennett, Valerie Plave. 1975. "Military Government in Mali." *Journal of Modern African Studies* 13 (2): 249–266.

Bergara, Mario, Witold J. Henisz, and Pablo Spiller. 1997. "Political Institutions and Electric Utility Investment: A Cross-National Analysis." *California Management Review* 40 (2): 18–35.

Betts, Richard K. 1981. "Surprise Despite Warning: Why Sudden Attacks Succeed." *Political Science Quarterly* 95 (4): 551–572.

Bienen, Henry. 1978. *Armies and Parties in Africa.* New York: African Publishing Company.

Bienen, Henry, and Nicolas van de Walle. 1989. "Time and Power in Africa." *American Political Science Review* 83 (1): 19–34.

Bienen, Henry, and Nicolas van de Walle. 1991. *Of Time and Power: Leadership Duration in the Modern World.* Stanford: Stanford University Press.

Black, Craig R. 2000. "Deterring Libya: The Strategic Culture of Muammar Qaddafi." Counter-Proliferation Papers, Future Warfare Series no. 8. Montgomery, AL: USAF Counter-Proliferation Center, Air War College.

Blaydes, Lisa. 2006. "Electoral Budget Cycles Under Authoritarianism: Economic Opportunism in Mubarek's Egypt." Presented at the Midwest Political Science Association annual meeting. Chicago, April 20–23.

Blimes, Randall J. 2006. "The Indirect Effect of Ethnic Heterogeneity on the Likelihood of Civil War Onset." *Journal of Conflict Resolution* 50 (4): 536–547.

Boix, Charles. 2003. *Democracy and Retribution.* New York: Cambridge University Press.

Box-Steffensmeier, Janet M., and Christopher J. W. Zorn. 2002. "Duration

Models and Proportional Hazards in Political Science." *American Journal of Political Science* 45: 951–967.

Branigan, William. 2003. "A Brief, Bitter War for Iraq's Military Officers." *Washington Post,* April 27.

Bratton, Michael, and Nicolas van de Walle. 1997. *Democratic Experiments in Africa: Regime Transitions in Comparative Perspective.* Cambridge: Cambridge University Press.

Braumoeller, Bear F. 2006. "Explaining Variance: Or, Stuck in a Moment We Can't Get Out Of." *Political Analysis* 14: 268–290.

Brooker, Paul. 2000. *Non-Democratic Regimes: Theory, Government, and Politics.* London: Macmillan.

Brown, D. S., and W. Hunter. 1999. "Democracy and Social Spending in Latin America, 1980–92." *American Political Science Review* 93 (4): 773–790.

Brownlee, Jason. 2008. "Bound to Rule: Party Institutions and Regime Trajectories in Malaysia and the Philippines." *Journal of East Asian Studies* 8: 89–118.

Budrauskaite, Alina, Jypara Mamytova, Katarina Mlinareviæ, and Alla Savina. 2002. "Trade Policy and Economic Growth: Cases of Belarus and Lithuania." *Privredna Kretanja i Ekonomska Politika* 90: 67–103.

Bueno de Mesquita, Bruce, and Randolph M. Siverson. 1995. "War and the Survival of Political Leaders: A Comparative Study of Regime Types and Political Accountability." *American Political Science Review* 89 (4): 841–855.

Bueno de Mesquita, Bruce, Alastair Smith, Randolph M. Siverson, and James D. Morrow. 2003. *The Logic of Political Survival.* Cambridge: Massachusetts Institute of Technology Press.

Carothers, Thomas. 2003. "Why Dictators Aren't Dominoes." *Foreign Policy,* July–August: 59–60.

Case, William. 1994. "The UMNO Party Election in Malaysia: One for the Money." *Asian Survey* 34 (10): 916–930.

Case, William. 1997. "The 1996 UMNO Party Election: 'Two for the Show.'" *Pacific Affairs* 70 (3): 393–411.

Case, William. 2002. *Politics in Southeast Asia: Democracy or Less.* Richmond, Surrey, UK: Curzon.

Celoza, Alberto F. 1997. *Ferdinand Marcos and the Philippines.* Westport: Greenwood.

"Chad: Coup Attempt Foiled, Government Says." 2006. *IRIN United National for the Coordination of Humanitarian Affairs,* March 15. www.irinnews.org/report.aspx?reportid=58438 (accessed December 8, 2008).

Cheng, Li, and Lynn White. 2003. "The Sixteenth Central Committee of the Chinese Communist Party: Hu Gets What?" *Asian Survey* 43 (4): 553–597.

Chiozza, Giacomo, and Henk E. Goemans. 2004. "International Conflict and the Tenure of Leaders: Is War Still Ex Post Inefficient?" *American Journal of Political Science* 48 (3): 604–619.

Clarke, Kevin A., and Randall Stone. 2008. "Democracy and the Logic of

Political Survival." *American Political Science Review* 102 (3): 387–392.

Congleton, Roger D. 1992. "Political Institutions and Pollution Control." *Review of Economics and Statistics* 74 (3): 412–421.

Costa Pinto, António. 2002. "Elites, Single Parties, and Political Decision-Making in Fascist Era Dictatorships." *Contemporary European History* 11 (3): 429–454.

Crassweller, Robert. 1966. *Trujillo: The Life and Times of a Caribbean Dictator.* New York: Macmillan.

Decalo, Samuel. 1976. *Coups and Army Rule in Africa: Studies in Military Style.* New Haven: Yale University Press.

Decalo, Samuel. 1985. "African Personal Dictatorships." *Journal of Modern African Studies* 23 (2): 209–237.

Decalo, Samuel. 1989. *Psychosis of Power.* Gainesville: Florida Academic Press.

"Democracy Index: Off the March." 2008. *The Economist,* October 29. www.economist.com/markets/rankings/displayStory.cfm?source= hptextfeature&story_id=12499352 (accessed November 18, 2008).

Diermeier, Daniel, and Keith Krehbiel. 2003. "Institutionalism as a Methodology." *Journal of Theoretical Politics* 15 (2): 123–144.

Dittmer, Lowell. 2003. "Leadership Change and Chinese Political Development." *China Quarterly* 176: 903–925.

Dolton, P. J., and G. H. Makepeace. 1987. "Interpreting Sample Selection Effects." *Economics Letters* 24: 373–379.

Downs, George W., and David M. Rocke. 1979. "Interpreting Heteroscedasticity." *American Journal of Political Science* 23 (4): 816–828.

Egorov, Georgy, and Konstantin Sonin. 2006. "Dictators and Their Viziers: Endogenizing the Loyalty-Competence Trade-Off." http://ssrn.com /abstract=630503 (accessed November 18, 2008).

Eisenstadt, Michael, and Kenneth M. Pollack. 2001. "Armies of Snow and Armies of Sand: The Impact of Soviet Military Doctrine on Arab Militaries." *Middle East Journal* 55 (4): 549–578.

"Europe's Last Dictatorship" 2006. *The Guardian,* March 2. www .guardian.co.uk/g2/story/0,,1721135,00.html (accessed December 9, 2008).

Eyerman, Joe, and Robert A. Hart Jr. 1996. "An Empirical Test of the Audience Cost Proposition: Democracy Speaks Louder Than Words." *Journal of Conflict Resolution* 40 (4): 597–616.

"Fall of Idi Amin." 1979. *Economic and Political Weekly,* May 26.

Farouk-Sluglett, Marion, and Peter Sluglett. 2002. *Iraq Since 1958: From Revolution to Dictatorship.* New York: Tauris.

Fatás, Antonio, and Ilian Mihov. 2005. "Policy Volatility, Institutions and Economic Growth." http://ssrn.com/abstract=887544 (accessed November 18, 2008).

Fearon, James. 1994. "Domestic Political Audiences and the Escalation of International Conflict." *American Political Science Review* 88 (3): 577–592.

Fearon, James. 1997. "Signaling Foreign Policy Interests: Tying Hands Versus Sinking Costs." *Journal of Conflict Resolution* 41 (1): 68–90.

Fearon, James, and David Laitin. 2003. "Ethnicity, Insurgency, and Civil War." *American Political Science Review* 97 (1): 75–90.

Feaver, Peter D. 1999. "Civil-Military Relations." *Annual Review of Political Science* 2: 211–241.

Ferguson, James. 1987. *Baby Doc and Papa Doc: Haiti and the Duvaliers*. Cambridge: Blackwell.

Ferguson, James. 1988. "Haiti from Dictatorship to Dictatorship." *Race and Class* 30: 23–40.

Finer, Samuel. 1962. *The Man on Horseback: The Role of the Military in Politics*. London: Pall Mall.

Finer, Samuel. 1975. "State and Nation-Building in Europe: The Role of the Military." In Charles Tilly (ed.), *The Formation of National States in Western Europe*. Princeton: Princeton University Press.

Fleishman, Jeffrey. 2004. "Ex-Baathists Offer US Advice, Await Call to Arms." *Los Angeles Times,* April 27.

Fox, John. 2002. "Cox Proportional-Hazards Regression for Survival Data." *R-Project.* http://cran.r-project.org/doc/contrib/Fox-Companion/appendix-cox-regression.pdf (accessed April 22, 2008).

Friedrich, Carl, and Zbigniew Brzezinski. 1956. *Totalitarian Dictatorship and Autocracy*. Cambridge: Harvard University Press.

Gallego, Maria, and Carolyn Pitchik. 2004. "An Economic Theory of Leadership Turnover." *Journal of Public Economics* 88 (12): 2361–2382.

Gandhi, Jennifer. 2008. "Dictatorial Institutions and Their Impact on Economic Growth." *European Journal of Sociology* (49): 3–30.

Gandhi, Jennifer, and Ellen Lust-Okar. 2009. "Elections Under Authoritarianism. *Annual Review of Political Science* 12: 403–422.

Gandhi, Jennifer, and Adam Przeworski. 2006. "Cooperation, Cooptation, and Rebellion Under Dictatorship." *Economics and Politics* 18 (1): 1–26.

Gandhi, Jennifer, and Adam Przeworski. 2007. "Authoritarian Institutions and the Survival of Autocrats." *Comparative Political Studies* 40 (11): 1279–1301.

Geddes, Barbara. 2003. *Paradigms and Sand Castles: Theory Building and Research Design in Comparative Politics*. Ann Arbor: University of Michigan Press.

Geddes, Barbara. 2004. "Minimum-Winning Coalitions and Personalization in Authoritarian Regimes." Presented at the American Political Science Association annual meeting. Chicago, September 2–5.

Geddes, Barbara. 2005. "Why Parties and Elections in Authoritarian Regimes?" Presented at the American Political Science Association annual meeting. Washington, DC, September 1–4.

Gelpi, Christopher, and Michael Griesdorf. 2001. "Winners or Losers? Democracies in International Crises, 1918–1994." *American Political Science Review* 95 (3): 633–647.

Gerstein, Remy. 2003. "Documents Show Urgent Iraqi Push to Recruit and Control Troops." *New York Times,* April 18.

Gleditsch, Kristian, and Erik Gartzke. 2007. "The Ties That Bias: Specifying and Operationalizing Components of Dyadic Dependence." Working Paper presented at the European Consortium for Political Research. Pisa, Italy, September 6–8.

Gleditsch, Nils Petter. 1999. "Do Open Windows Encourage Conflict?" *Statsvetenskaplig Tidskrift* 102 (3): 333–343.

Goemans, Hein. 1995. "The Causes of War Termination: Domestic Politics and War Aims." PhD thesis. University of Chicago, Department of Political Science.

Goemans, Hein, Kristian Skrede Gleditsch, and Giacomo Chiozza. 2007. "Case Description File: June 2007." *Archigos: A Data Set of Leaders, 1875–2004.* http://mail.rochester.edu/~hgoemans/CaseDescription June2007.pdf (accessed April 22, 2008).

Gould, David J. 1980. *Bureaucratic Corruption and Underdevelopment in the Third World: The Case of Zaire.* New York: Pergamon.

Gowa, Joanne. 1995. "Democratic States and International Disputes." *International Organization* 49 (3): 511–522.

Granville, Johanna. 2006. "East Germany in 1956: Walter Ulbricht's Tenacity in the Face of Opposition." *Australian Journal of Political Science* 52 (3): 417–438.

Greene, William. 2000. *Econometric Analysis.* 4th ed. Upper Saddle River, NJ: Prentice Hall.

Grieder, Peter. 2000. *The East German Leadership, 1946–73: Conflict and Crisis.* Manchester: Manchester University Press.

Gugliotta, Guy. 1986. "The Inner Workings of Dictatorship." *APF Reporter* 9 (2): http://aliciapatterson.org/APF0902/Gugliotta/Gugliotta.html (accessed April 22, 2008).

Gunter, Michael M. 2001. "Qaddafi Reconsidered." *Journal of Conflict Studies* 21 (1): 122–131.

Haber, Stephen. 2006. "Authoritarian Government." In Barry Weingast and Donald Wittman (eds.), *The Oxford Handbook of Political Economy.* Oxford: Oxford University Press.

Haggard, Stephen. 1988. "The Philippines: Picking Up After Marcos." In Raymond Vernon (ed.), *The Promise of Privatization.* New York: New York Council for Foreign Relations.

Haggard, Stephen, and Richard Kaufman. 1995. *The Political Economy of Democratic Transitions.* Princeton: Princeton University Press.

Halvorsen, Robert, and Raymond Palmquist. 1980. "The Interpretation of Dummy Variables in Semilogarithmic Equations." *American Economic Review* 70 (3): 474–475.

Handel, Michael. 1989. *Leaders and Intelligence.* London: Taylor and Francis.

"'A Happy Ending': Gaddafi Son Hails Nurses Accord." 2007. *Reuters,* July 30. http://africa.reuters.com/wire/news/usnL30136235.html (accessed November 14, 2008).

Harden, Blaine. 1987. "Zaire's President Mobutu Sese Seko: Political Craftsman Worth Billions." *Washington Post,* December 27.

Hartlyn, Jonathan. 1998. *The Struggle for Democratic Politics in the Dominican Republic.* Chapel Hill: University of North Carolina Press.

Harvey, Andrew. 1976. "Estimating Regression Models with Multiplicative Heteroskedasticity." *Econometrica* 44 (3): 461–465.

Hawes, Gary. 1995. "Marcos, His Cronies, and the Philippines' Failure to Develop." In John Ravenhill (ed.), *Singapore, Indonesia, Malaysia, the Philippines, and Thailand.* Aldershot: Elgar.

Heckman, James. 1979. "Selection Bias as a Specification Error." *Econometrica* 47 (1): 153–161.

Henisz, Witold. 2000. "The Institutional Environment for Multinational Investment." *Journal of Law, Economics, and Organization* 16 (2): 334–364.

Henisz, Witold. 2004. "Political Institutions and Policy Volatility." *Economics and Politics* 16 (1): 1–27.

Herz, John. 1950. "Idealist Internationalism and the Security Dilemma." *World Politics* 2 (2): 157–174.

Higley, John, and Michael G. Burton. 1989. "The Elite Variable in Democratic Transitions and Breakdowns." *American Sociological Review* 54 (1): 17–32.

Honaker, James, Anne Joseph, Gary King, Kenneth Scheve, and Naunihal Singh. 1999. "*Amelia:* A Program for Missing Data." http://GKing.Harvard.edu (accessed April 22, 2008).

Howe, Herbert. 2001. *Ambiguous Order: Military Forces in African States.* Boulder: Lynne Rienner.

Huber, P. J. 1967. "The Behavior of Maximum Likelihood Estimates Under Non-Standard Conditions." *Proceedings of the Fifth Berkeley Symposium on Mathematical Statistics and Probability* 4: 221–233.

Hunt, Benjamin. 2002. "The Macroeconomic Effects of Higher Oil Prices." *National Institute Economic Review* 179 (1): 87–103.

"Iraqi Information Minister Denies Presence of US Forces in Baghdad." 2003. *Foreign Broadcast Information Service,* April 7.

"Iraq's al-Sahhaf Holds News Conference on Military Situation." 2003. *Doha al-Jazirah News,* March 31.

Ireland, Michael J., and Scott Sigmund Gartner. 2001. "Time to Fight: Government Type and Conflict Initiation in Parliamentary Systems." *Journal of Conflict Resolution* 45 (5): 547–568.

Jackman, Robert W. 1978. "The Predictability of Coups d'État: A Model with African Data." *American Political Science Review* 72 (4): 1262–1275.

Jackson, Robert H., and Carl G. Rosberg. 1982. *Personal Rule in Black Africa: Prince, Autocrat, Prophet, Tyrant.* Berkeley: University of California Press.

Jensen, Nathan M. 2003. "Multinational Corporations: Political Regimes and Inflows of Foreign Direct Investment." *International Organization* 57 (3): 587–616.

Jervis, Robert. 1978. "Cooperation Under the Security Dilemma." *World Politics* 30 (2): 167–214.

Johnson, Thomas, Robert Slater, and Pat McGowan. 1984. "Explaining African Military Coups d'État, 1960–1982." *American Political Science Review* 78 (3): 622–640.

Jones, Daniel M., Stuart A. Bremer, and J. David Singer. 1996. "Militarized Interstate Disputes, 1816–1992: Rationale, Coding Rules, and Empirical Patterns." *Conflict Management and Peace Science* 15 (2): 163–215.

Kebschull, H. G. 1994. "Operation 'Just Missed': Lessons from Failed Coup Attempts." *Armed Forces and Society* 20 (4): 565–579.

Keefer, Philip, and Stephen Knack. 1997. "Does Social Capital Have an Economic Payoff? A Cross-Country Investigation." *Quarterly Journal of Economics* 112 (4): 1251–1288.

Keele, Luke, and David K. Park. 2004. "Difficult Choices: An Evaluation of Heterogeneous Choice Models." Presented at the American Political Science Association annual meeting. Chicago, September 2–5.

Kendall, Diana. 2006. *Sociology in Our Times: The Essentials*. Florence, KY: Cengage Learning.

Kennedy, G. 1974. *The Military in the Third World*. New York: Scribner.

Kiernan, Ben. 2004. *How Pol Pot Came to Power: Colonialism, Nationalism, and Communism in Cambodia, 1930–1975*. New Haven: Yale University Press.

Kind, Hans. 2000. "The Philippines: The Sick Man of Asia: Economic Development in the Philippines After 1946." Working Paper no. 24, May. http://hdl.handle.net/2330/1235 (accessed December 23, 2008).

King, Gary. 1989. *Unifying Political Methodology: The Likelihood Theory of Statistical Inference*. Cambridge: Cambridge University Press.

King, Gary, James Honaker, Anne Joseph, and Kenneth Scheve. 2001. "Analyzing Incomplete Political Science Data: An Alternative Algorithm for Multiple Imputation." *American Political Science Review* 95 (1): 49–69.

King, Gary, Michael Tomz, and Jason Wittenberg. 2000. "Making the Most of Statistical Analysis: Improving Interpretation and Presentation." *American Journal of Political Science* 44 (2): 347–361.

Kinne, Brandon J. 2005. "Decision Making in Autocratic Regimes: A Poliheuristic Perspective." *International Studies Perspectives* 6: 114–128.

Klieman, Aaron S. 1980. "Confined to Barracks: Emergencies and the Military in Developing Societies." *Comparative Politics* 12 (2): 143–163.

Koh, C. 2000. "Why the Military Obeys the Party's Orders to Repress Popular Uprisings: The Chinese Military." *Issues & Studies* 36 (6): 27–51.

Koh, David. 2001. "The Politics of a Divided Party and Parkinson's State in Vietnam." *Contemporary Southeast Asia* 23 (3): 533–552.

Kposowa, Augustin, and J. Craig Jenkins. 1993. "The Structural Sources of Military Coups in Post-Colonial Africa, 1957–1984." *American Journal of Sociology* 99 (1): 126–163.

Kugler, Jack, and Yi Feng. 1999. "Explaining and Modeling Democratic Transitions." *Journal of Conflict Resolution* 43 (2): 139–146.

Kurizaki, Shuhei. 2007. "Efficient Secrecy: Public Versus Private Threats in Crisis Diplomacy." *American Political Science Review* 101 (3): 543–558.

Lai, Brian, and Dan Slater. 2006. "Institutions of the Offensive: Domestic Sources of Dispute Initiation in Authoritarian Regimes, 1950–1992." *American Journal of Political Science* 50 (1): 113–126.

Lake, D. A., and M. Baum. 2001. "The Invisible Hand of Democracy: Political Control and the Provision of Public Services." *Comparative Political Studies* 34 (6): 587–621.

Legum, Colin (ed.). 1975–1976. *Africa Contemporary Record*. Teaneck, NJ: Holmes & Meier.

Legum, Colin. 1997. "Behind the Clown's Mask." *Transition* 75: 250–258.

Lemke, Douglas. 2002. *Regions of War and Peace*. Cambridge: Cambridge University Press.

Leslie, Winsome J. 1987. *The World Bank and Structural Adjustment in Developing Countries: The Case of Zaire*. Boulder: Lynne Rienner.

Levy, Jack, and Mike Froelick. 1985. "The Causes of the Iran-Iraq War." In James Brown and William P. Snyder (eds.), *The Regionalization of War*. New Brunswick, NJ: Transaction.

Lewis, Paul H. 1978. "Salazar's Ministerial Elite, 1932–1968." *Journal of Politics* 40 (3): 622–647.

Londregan, John B., and Keith Poole. 1990. "Poverty, the Coup Trap, and the Seizure of Executive Power." *World Politics* 42 (2): 151–183.

Londregan, John B., and Keith Poole. 1996. "Does High Income Promote Democracy?" *World Politics* 49 (1): 1–30.

Lopez-Calvo, Ignacio. 2005. *"God and Trujillo": Literary and Cultural Representations of the Dominican Dictator*. Gainesville: University of Florida Press.

Lust-Okar, Ellen. 2005. *Structuring Conflict in the Arab World: Incumbents, Opponents, and Institutions*. Cambridge: Cambridge University Press.

Magaloni, Beatriz. 2006. *Voting for Autocracy: Hegemonic Party Survival and Its Demise in Mexico*. Cambridge: Cambridge University Press.

Magaloni, Beatriz. 2008. "Credible Power-Sharing and the Longevity of Authoritarian Rule." *Comparative Political Studies* 41 (4–5): 715–741.

Magaloni, Beatriz, and Ruth Kricheli. 2010. "Political Order and One-Party Rule." *Annual Review of Political Science* 13: 123–143.

Manski, Charles F. 1999. *Identification Problems in the Social Sciences*. Cambridge: Harvard University Press.

Marinov, Nikolay. 2005. "Do Economic Sanctions Destabilize Country Leaders?" *American Journal of Political Science* 49 (3): 564–576.

Marr, Phebe. 1985. *The Modern History of Iraq*. Boulder: Westview.

McAdams, A. James. 1985. *East Germany and Détente: Building Authority After the Wall*. Cambridge: Cambridge University Press.

McVey, Ruth Thomas. 1992. *Southeast Asian Capitalists*. Ithaca: SEAP.

Montes, Manuel. 1988. "The Business Sector and Development Policies." In Alichir Ishii et al. (eds.), *National Development Policies and the Business Sector in the Philippines*. Tokyo: Institute of Developing Economies.

Moya Pons, Frank. 1995. *The Dominican Republic: A National History.* New Rochelle: Hispaniola.

Mulligan, Casey B., Ricard Gil, and Xavier Sala-i-Martin. 2004. "Do Democracies Have Different Public Policies Than Nondemocracies?" *Journal of Economic Perspectives* 18 (1): 51–74.

Mulvey, Charles. 1978. *The Economic Analysis of Trade Unions.* Oxford: Robinson.

Mutalib, Hussin. 2000. "Illiberal Democracy and the Future of Opposition in Singapore." *Third World Quality* 21 (2): 313–342.

Nathan, Andrew. 1973. "A Factional Model for CCP Politics." *China Quarterly* 53: 34–66.

O'Kane, Rosemary. 1989. "Military Regimes: Power and Force." *European Journal of Political Science* 17: 333–350.

Olson, Mancur. 2000. *Power and Prosperity: Outgrowing Communist and Capitalist Dictatorships.* Oxford: Oxford University Press.

Partell, Peter J., and Glenn Palmer. 1999. "Audience Costs and Interstate Crises: An Empirical Assessment of Fearon's Model of Dispute Outcomes." *International Studies Quarterly* 43 (2): 389–405.

Peceny, Mark, Caroline C. Beer, and Shannon Sanchez-Terry. 2002. "Dictatorial Peace?" *American Political Science Review* 96 (2): 15–26.

Peceny, Mark, and Christopher K. Butler. 2004. "The Conflict Behavior of Authoritarian Regimes." *International Politics* 41 (4): 565–581.

Perlmutter, Amos. 1981. *Modern Authoritarianism: A Comparative Institutional Analysis.* New Haven: Yale University Press.

Perry, William J. 1991. "Desert Storm and Deterrence." *Foreign Affairs* 70 (4): 66–82.

Pike, Douglas. 1989. "Origins of Leadership Change in the Socialist Republic of Vietnam." In Raymond C. Taras (ed.), *Leadership Change in Communist States.* Boston: Unwin Hyman.

Polity IV Project. 2007. "Political Regime Characteristics and Transitions, 1800–2006." www.systemicpeace.org/polity/polity4.htm (accessed April 22, 2008).

Pollack, Kenneth M. 2002. *The Threatening Storm: The Case for Invading Iraq.* New York: Random.

Post, Jerrold M. 1991. "Saddam Hussein of Iraq: A Political Psychology Profile." Case Western Reserve University School of Law. http://law.case.edu/saddamtrial/documents/saddam_hussein_political _psychology_profile.pdf (accessed December 9, 2008).

Post, Jerrold M., and Amatzia Baram. 2002. "Saddam Is Iraq: Iraq Is Saddam (Until Operation Iraqi Freedom)." In Barry R. Schneider and Jerrold M. Post (eds.), *Know Thy Enemy: Profiles of Adversary Leaders and Their Strategic Cultures.* Washington, DC: US Government Printing Office.

Poterba, James. 1994. "State Responses to Fiscal Crises: The Effects of Budgetary Institutions and Politics." *Journal of Political Economy* 102: 799–821.

Prins, Brandon C. 2003. "Institutional Instability and the Credibility of Audience Costs: Political Participation and Interstate Crisis Bargaining, 1816–1992." *Journal of Peace Research* 40 (1): 67–84.

Przeworski, Adam, Michael E. Alvarez, Jose Antonio Cheibub, and Fernando Limongi. 2000. *Democracy and Development: Political Institutions and Well-Being in the World, 1950–1990.* Cambridge: Cambridge University Press.

Raknerud, Arvid, and Havard Hegre. 1997. "The Hazard of War: Reassessing the Evidence for the Democratic Peace." *Journal of Peace Research* 34 (4): 385–404.

Ramsay, Kristopher W. 2004. "Politics at the Water's Edge: Crisis Bargaining and Electoral Competition." *Journal of Conflict Resolution* 98 (4): 459–486.

Ravenhill, F. J. 1974. "Military Rule in Uganda: The Politics of Survival." *African Studies Review* 17 (1): 229–260.

Reed, William. 2003a. "Information and Economic Interdependence." *Journal of Conflict Resolution* 47 (1): 54–71.

Reed, William. 2003b. "Information, Power, and War." *American Political Science Review* 97 (3): 633–641.

Reiter, Dan, and Allan C. Stam. 2003. "Identifying the Culprit: Democracy, Dictatorship, and Dispute Initiation." *American Political Science Review* 97 (3): 333–337.

Remmer, Karen L. 1986. "Exclusionary Democracy." *Studies in Comparative International Development* 20 (4): 64–85.

Remmer, Karen L. 1991. *Military Rule in Latin America.* Boulder: Westview.

Reuter, Ora John, and Thomas F. Remington. 2009. "Dominant Party Regimes and the Commitment Problem: The Case of United Russia." *Comparative Political Studies* 42: 501–525.

Rindova, Violina P., and William H. Starbuck. 1997. "Distrust in Dependence: The Ancient Challenge of Superior-Subordinate Relations." In T. A. R. Clark (ed.), *Advancement of Organization Behavior: Essays in Honor of Derek Pugh.* Hanover, NH: Dartmouth College.

Roeder, Phillip G. 1993. *Red Sunset: The Failure of Soviet Politics.* Princeton: Princeton University Press.

Romer, D. 1993. "Openness and Inflation: Theory and Evidence." *Quarterly Journal of Economics* 108 (4): 869–903.

Sanhueza, Ricardo. 1999. "The Hazard Rate of Political Regimes." *Public Choice* 98 (3–4): 337–367.

Sarotte, M. E. 2001. *Dealing with the Devil: East Germany, Détente, and Ostpolitk, 1969–1973.* Chapel Hill: University of North Carolina Press.

Schatzberg, Michael G. 1988. *The Dialectics of Oppression in Zaire.* Bloomington: Indiana University Press.

Schofield, Matthew. 2006. "Saddam Never Planned Insurgency: US Military Study." *Agence France Presse,* March 14.

Schultz, Kenneth A. 1998. "Domestic Opposition and Signaling in International Crises." *American Political Science Review* 92 (4): 829–844.

Schultz, Kenneth A. 1999. "Do Domestic Institutions Constrain or Inform? Contrasting Two Institutional Perspectives on Democracy and War." *International Organization* 52 (2): 233–266.

Schultz, Kenneth A. 2001. "Looking for Audience Costs." *Journal of Conflict Resolution* 45 (1): 32–60.

Siegel, Eric. 1997. "I Know That You Know, and You Know That I Know: An Information Theory of the Democratic Peace." Presented at the American Political Science Association annual meeting. Washington, DC, August 28–31.

Silitski, Vitali. 2005. "Preempting Democracy: The Case of Belarus." *Journal of Democracy* 16 (4): 83–97.

Simons, Geoff. 1996. *Libya: The Struggle for Survival.* New York: St. Martin's.

Singer, J. David, Stuart Bremer, and John Stuckey. 1972. "Capability Distribution, Uncertainty, and Major Power War, 1820–1965." In Bruce Russett (ed.), *Peace, War, and Numbers.* Beverly Hills: Sage.

Slantchev, Branislav L. 2006. "Politicians, the Media, and Domestic Audience Costs." *International Studies Quarterly* 50 (2): 445–477.

Smith, Alastair. 1998. "International Crises and Domestic Politics." *American Political Science Review* 92 (3): 623–638.

Smith, Benjamin. 2005. "Life of the Party: The Origins of Regime Breakdown and Persistence Under Single-Party Rule." *World Politics* 57: 421–451.

Snyder, Richard. 1992. "Explaining Transitions from Neo-patrimonial Dictatorships." *Comparative Politics* 24 (4): 379–399.

Svolik, Milan. 2009. "Power Sharing and Leadership Dynamics in Authoritarian Regimes." *American Journal of Political Science* 53 (2): 477–494.

Tamada, Yoshifumi. 1995. "Coups in Thailand, 1980–1991: Classmates, Internal Conflicts, and Relations with the Government of the Military." *Southeast Asian Studies* 33 (3): 317–339.

Tanzi, Vito. 1986. "Public Expenditure and Public Debt." In John Bristow and Declan McDonagh (eds.), *Public Expenditure: The Key Issues.* Dublin: Institute of Public Administration.

Therneau, Terry M., and Patricia M. Grambsch. 2000. *Modeling Survival Data: Extending the Cox Model.* New York: Springer-Verlag.

Titley, Brian. 1997. *Dark Age: The Political Odyssey of Emperor Bokassa.* Liverpool: Liverpool University Press.

Tomz, Michael. 2007. "Domestic Audience Costs in International Relations: An Experimental Approach." *International Organization* 61 (4): 821–840.

Toset, Hans Petter Wollebaek, Nils Petter Gleditsch, and Havard Hegre. 2000. "Shared Rivers and Interstate Conflict." *Political Geography* 19 (6): 971–996.

Treisman, Daniel. 2000. "Decentralization and Inflation: Commitment, Collective Action, or Continuity?" *American Political Science Review* 94 (4): 837–858.

Tsebelis, George. 2002. *Veto Players: How Political Institutions Work.* Princeton: Princeton University Press.

Tullock, Gordon. 1987. *Autocracy.* Boston: Kluwer Academic.

Turner, Thomas. 1988. "Decline or Recovery in Zaire." *Current History* 87 (529): 213–216.

Unger, Jonathan, and Lowell Dittmer. 2002. *The Nature of Chinese Politics.* Armonk, NY: Sharpe.

US Department of Defense. 2000. "Operation Desert Shield/Desert Storm Timeline." http://osd.dtic.mil/news/Aug2000/n08082000_20008088 .html (accessed December 7, 2008).

Van Doorn, J. (ed.). 1968. *Armed Forces and Society: Sociological Essays.* The Hague: Mouton.

Viorst, Milton. 1999. "The Colonel in His Labyrinth." *Foreign Affairs,* March–April: 60–75.

Waltz, Kenneth. 1959. *Man, the State, and War.* New York: Columbia University Press.

Weeks, Jessica. 2008. "Autocratic Audience Costs: Regime Type and Signaling Resolve." *International Organization* 62 (1): 35–64.

Whitson, William. 1969. "The Field Army in Chinese Communist Military Politics." *China Quarterly* 37: 1–30.

Wiarda, Howard. 1968. *Dictatorship and Development: The Methods of Control in Trujillo's Dominican Republic.* Gainesville: University of Florida Press.

Williams, Richard. 2006. "Using Heterogeneous Choice Models to Compare Logit and Probit Coefficients Across Groups." Unpublished manuscript.

Wilson, Sven E., and Daniel M. Butler. 2007. "A Lot More to Do: The Sensitivity of Time-Series Cross-Section Analyses to Simple Alternative Specifications." *Political Analysis* 15 (2): 101–123.

Wintrobe, Ronald. 1998. *The Political Economy of Dictatorship.* Cambridge: Cambridge University Press.

Woods, Kevin, James Lacey, and Williamson Murray. 2006. "Saddam's Delusions: The View from the Inside." *Foreign Affairs,* May–June: 2–26.

Woods, Kevin, and Michael Pease. 2006. *The Iraqi Perspectives Report.* Annapolis, MD: Naval Institute Press.

Woods, Kevin, Michael Pease, Mark Stout, Williamson Murray, and James Lacey. 2006. "Iraqi Perspectives Report: A View of Operation Iraqi Freedom from Saddam's Senior Leadership." Report no. A503644. Norfolk, VA: US Joint Forces Command.

World Bank. 2003. *World Development Indicators 2003.* Washington, DC.

Wright, Joseph. 2008. "Do Authoritarian Institutions Constrain? How Legislatures Affect Economic Growth and Investment." *American Journal of Political Science* 52 (2): 322–343.

Yatchew, A., and Z. Griliches. 1985. "Specification Error in Probit Models." *Review of Economics and Statistics* 18 (3): 134–139.

Index

About the Book

In comparison to democratic political systems, we know very little about how dictatorships work. Who are the key political actors? Where does the locus of power rest? What determines leadership behavior—and survival?

Erica Frantz and Natasha Ezrow argue that dictatorships are not regimes driven by the whims of a single individual. Frantz and Ezrow reveal how leader-elite relations are strongly influenced by the nature of the political institutions in a regime, and in turn how those relations profoundly affect both domestic and foreign policy. Combining cross-national quantitative analyses with a selection of case studies, they uniquely explore the internal architecture of authoritarian government.

Erica Frantz is a political analyst at the Institute for Physical Sciences in Washington, DC. **Natasha Ezrow** is lecturer in the Department of Government at the University of Essex.